Shruthi Rao (http://shruthi-rao.com) is an author and editor. She has a master's degree in energy engineering, and worked in the IT industry before she started writing. She is the author of *Susie Will Not Speak* (2018, Duckbill), *Manya Learns to Roar* (2017, Duckbill), *The Secret Garden* (2016, NSI), *Avani and the Pea Plant* (2016, Pratham) among others. She loves books, desserts, trees, benches, science and long walks. Shruthi is obsessed with learning about new things, and believes that there is always more to everything than meets the eye

20 INDIANS Who Changed the World

SHRUTHI RAO

talking CUB
An Imprint of Speaking Tiger

TALKING CUB
Speaking Tiger Books LLP
125 A, Ground Floor Shahpur Jat, Near Asiad Village
New Delhi 110049

Published in paperback in Talking Cub by Speaking Tiger
in 2019

ISBN: 978-93-88874-70-0
eISBN: 978-93-88874-71-7

10 9 8 7 6 5 4 3 2

Typeset in Adobe Gandhi Serif by Jojy Philip
Printed at Shree Maitrey Printech Pvt. Ltd., Noida

contents

India's Contribution to the World

Introduction

FOR MILLENNIA, THE INDIAN SUBCONTINENT HAS been a vibrant hub of activity. A major centre for trade and learning, it has attracted merchants, scholars and travellers from all over the world—and invaders too! India has exerted significant influence in the way that people around the world eat, the clothes they wear, the things they learn, study and think about, and what they do for fun.

But who do we credit for India making its mark on the world? For the most part, those responsible have been unknown and nameless people—for instance, farmers who grew cotton and spices that were prized around the world, weavers who produced beautiful textiles, artisans who made precious artefacts, scholars who made significant advancement in literature, science, mathematics and medicine, and the traders and merchants who took these products and ideas along with them on their journeys around the world.

But in some instances, we know exactly who it was that introduced an idea or made a discovery that changed the world. In this book, you will find twenty such Indians.

There have, of course, been many more remarkable Indians who have done much for the country, and whose work has improved the lives of Indians. But the effects of their work have mostly remained within the borders of India. The twenty personalities in this book have been chosen because of the impact their work has had internationally.

But what is the definition of an Indian? Some of the personalities in this book have spent most of their lives outside India, and are not Indian citizens any more. On the other hand, some were born outside India. But, at some point in their lives, all the people in this book have identified as Indian.

The work of a few of the people in this book might be considered controversial by some. Be that as it may, they have had a considerable influence on the world and so, have earned a place in this book.

This is in no way a complete list of all the Indians who have changed the world. Some readers are bound to feel that one or the other famous name should have been included. I'd love to hear from you about them, and why you think they changed the world.

buddha

c. 563–c. 483 BCE

Who: The founder of Buddhism.

How he changed the world: The teachings of the Buddha and the way of life he preached are known as Buddhism. It is practised all over the world. Buddhists form the majority in a number of countries in Asia, and Buddhism is widespread in the US and Europe too. It has influenced other religions, as well as art, literature and philosophy. Nearly 500 million people around the world practice Buddhism today.

THE BUDDHA WAS BORN SIDDHARTHA GAUTAMA IN 6th century BCE in Lumbini, in present-day Nepal. His father Suddhodana, of the Shakya clan, ruled from his capital Kapilavastu.

When Siddhartha was born, a holy man visited the palace. One look at the baby, and the holy man prophesied that Siddhartha would grow up to be either a great king, or a holy man.

Siddhartha's father had no doubts about what *he* wanted his son to be—a king of course, the successor to the throne. So, he tried his best to make sure that Siddhartha lived a sheltered, luxurious life. He instructed the young boy in matters of the state, good governance and warfare, and everything required to be a good ruler. But like a typical parent, he was worried about 'wrong influences', and he kept Siddhartha away from the hardships of life. He went to extremes and even forbade Siddhartha to step out of the palace premises.

At sixteen, Siddhartha was married to Yashodhara, and some years later, they had a son, Rahula. Everything seemed to be going just as Suddhodana wanted.

But (of course there's a 'but'), who would want to be cooped up inside all the time? Siddhartha became increasingly dissatisfied and restless. He started giving his father the slip and directed his charioteer Channa to take him on trips out of the palace grounds. On his secret excursions, he saw what his father hadn't wanted him to see—poverty, sickness, suffering and death. Siddhartha was disturbed by what he saw. He couldn't get those images out of his head.

On one such outing, he spotted an ascetic, and Siddhartha could see from the ascetic's expression and demeanour that he was completely at peace. Channa explained to Siddhartha that an ascetic was a person who had renounced the world, and had given up all worldly delights. Siddhartha decided that he wanted some of that peace, and if asceticism was the way, then so be it.

One night, Siddhartha stole out of his room, leaving his sleeping wife and son behind. He left the palace and took to the streets. He donned the simple robes of an ascetic, and cut off his hair. He roamed around the land, homeless, and begged for his food. He spent years travelling across India and approached well-known gurus of the time, became their disciple, and learnt and practiced meditation. He starved himself, subjected himself to pain, held his breath for long durations, didn't sleep for days, hoping that punishing himself like this would lead him to the 'truth'.

Then, one day, as the story goes, Siddhartha was close to collapsing with exhaustion, when a girl offered him a bowl of sweet rice. He accepted it and put the bowl to his lips. The delicious sweet trickled into him and rejuvenated him. Suddenly, it dawned on him that this kind of hardship and denying his body nourishment wouldn't serve any purpose. It wasn't the way to achieve what he wanted. He concluded that life should be lived in moderation. He decided that he would follow the 'Middle Path': neither extreme luxury, nor extreme poverty.

Siddhartha now had a new sense of purpose. He continued travelling, reached Gaya (in present-day Bihar) where he sat under a peepul tree and meditated for days. And then, on the forty-ninth day, he was Enlightened, and came to be known as the Buddha (The Enlightened/Awakened One).

But what exactly is enlightenment? There are various interpretations and explanations of what exactly happened when Siddhartha attained enlightenment. But in short, it probably just meant that he was able to see the world with new eyes, and that he found the answers to the questions he was looking for about how to live life.

The Four Noble Truths

First Noble Truth: Suffering exists.

Second Noble Truth: The three main reasons for suffering are desire or craving, ignorance, hatred.

Third Noble Truth: Suffering can be ended.

Fourth Noble Truth: The way to end suffering is by following the Eight-fold Path, i.e., right views/understanding, right thoughts, right speech, right action, right livelihood, right effort, right mindfulness, and right concentration.

Then, he put this awareness into simple words, and started teaching them as the Four Noble Truths and the Eight-fold Path, and led other people towards enlightenment.

Word of his teachings spread. Men and women from all walks and classes of life became his disciples. Some of them became monks, and they themselves travelled across India spreading the teachings of the Buddha. Monasteries and prayers halls were built, and sanghas (Buddhist communities) were established all over the country.

The principles of Buddhism really appealed to people. For one, it was an enticing thought that individuals could become enlightened in this very life, and that they need not wait until they died to achieve salvation (to be freed from ignorance and the effects of sin). Besides, Buddhism, unlike Hinduism, had no caste system: it welcomed everybody with open arms. So, scores of people turned to Buddhism for comfort.

The Buddha died at the age of eighty, but his disciples passed on his teachings to the following generations.

In the 3rd century BCE, Buddhism got a major shot in the arm. The powerful Mauryan emperor Ashoka, disillusioned by a bloody battle, embraced Buddhism and spread its principles all around the country. This was the Golden Age of Buddhism. Ashoka sent missionaries to Sri Lanka too, and word about Buddhism spread out of the country for the first time. The Sri Lankan king converted to Buddhism, and established a sangha. He took holy relics from India, including a cutting from the sacred bodhi tree (the peepul tree under which the Buddha was enlightened). The tree is believed to be still growing in Anuradhapura, where he had planted it.

In the following centuries, Buddhism continued to spread to the neighbouring countries. International Buddhist councils were held to discuss, collect and organize the teachings of the Buddha. At one such council, different opinions arose about what the Buddha actually taught, and Buddhism split into two main schools of thought: Theravada and Mahayana. Mahayana spread northwards, to Nepal, Tibet, China, Vietnam and Korea. Theravada moved south to Sri Lanka, Thailand and Myanmar.

These schools of thought are practiced in these regions to this day.

Buddhists from other countries too came to India to learn more about their faith. They had to make dangerous journeys to reach India. Many of them such as the Chinese scholars Faxian and Xuanzang wrote travelogues which now serve as invaluable sources of information about Indian history and lifestyle in that era.

Buddhism reached China in the 1st century CE, probably through the Silk Route. By the 6th century CE, it became one of the three main religions of China, along with Taoism and Confucianism. People were attracted to its teachings about suffering, rebirth and nirvana. Donations poured in, and temples and monasteries were built, which became important centres of teaching, charity and studies.

Buddhism spread as far as Japan through Korea and China. It reached Thailand, probably through traders. It has been the official religion of Thailand for nearly 800 years now. More than 90 per cent of Thailand's population consists of Buddhists. Buddhism is the official religion of Laos and Cambodia too.

Buddhism has also influenced the art and architecture of several countries. Some of the most beautiful monuments around Asia are Buddhist structures. There are statues and paintings of Buddha from China, Korea, Japan, and of course India, each in its typical local style. In China, Greek and Indian styles blended with Chinese aesthetics, and an entirely different kind of art was born.

Buddhism mingled with existing religions and cultures and took on new forms. In India, the Buddha was absorbed into Hinduism around 10th century CE, and was included as one of the ten avatars of Lord Vishnu. Scholars also believe that vegetarianism became a part of Hinduism because of the influence of Buddhism.

Different schools of Buddhism arose too—for instance, the Zen school of Buddhism. It was founded by an Indian monk Bodhidharma and spread from China to Japan.

Until about a century ago, Buddhism was largely limited to Asia. But gradually, as Buddhist texts were translated into Western languages, and as Buddhists migrated to the West, Buddhism spread its wings and made its way to Europe and the United States.

Buddhism became very popular in the West mainly because of the surge of peace movements in the 1970s. The ideas behind these movements went hand in hand with Buddhist principles. Besides, Buddhism has an informal structure and a welcoming nature, thus making it easy to get drawn to it. Also, there is a growing concern around the globe about the state of our planet and how humans are harming it. The Buddhist attitudes of peace, mindfulness and care for living beings tend to make people believe that Buddhism could be the solution to the problems of the earth. It also helped that a large number of celebrities publicly claimed to have converted to Buddhism, making it an attractive religion.

The 14th Dalai Lama is probably the best-known Buddhist today, and a popular figure. He is known largely for his advocacy of Buddhism and is the spiritual leader of the people of Tibet.

panini

5th century BCE

Who: A Sanskrit scholar and grammarian

How he changed the world: His work on grammar laid the foundation for the study of linguistics throughout the world. It also formed the basis for the principles of computer programming.

About 2500 years ago, there lived a bright little boy. One day, a palmist visited the boy and his parents. He took the boy's small palm in his, and examined the lines on it, saying that he would predict the boy's future.

The palmist shook his head with regret. 'The boy doesn't have an education line at all,' he said to the parents. 'He will remain illiterate all his life.'

The parents were aghast. They had been certain that the boy was clever and had an illustrious future as a scholar.

The boy said, 'Where is the line supposed to be?'

The palmist pointed out the education line on his own palm.

The boy nodded. He went inside, picked up a knife, and carved a line on his palm. He went up to the palmist and held out his palm. 'Now do I have an education line?' he asked.

The boy was Panini, who went on to become one of the greatest scholars in the world.

This is probably an apocryphal story (a made-up story widely believed to be true). But what we know for sure is that Panini indeed existed, and that he was a distinguished scholar. The effects of his work on grammar are being seen and felt even today.

The Vedas are about 4000 years old. They are India's most ancient works. Some believe they are of divine origin. So, naturally, the ancient sages and scholars were very particular about the Vedas being recited correctly, so that their sanctity could be preserved.

But it wasn't an easy task. First of all, it was in Sanskrit, and if you've tried reciting a Sanskrit shloka, you'll know that your tongue has to do gymnastics to get the pronunciation just right. But that is not all. It wasn't only the words of the Vedas that were important. One had to recite them with the correct pitch, intonation and in the right metre. Besides, these works were rarely written down. They were passed down from generation to generation orally. And we're talking about thousands of verses! So, no matter how careful you were, mistakes invariably crept in. And sometimes these mistakes could change the meaning of the entire verse. (If you've played Chinese Whispers, you'll know how that would turn out!)

Thus, it became necessary to have an ironclad system of grammar and phonetics so that rules could be laid down for the right pronunciation. If you followed these rules, there would be lesser chance of making mistakes. And that is probably why the science of linguistics developed so early in ancient India—sages and scholars believed they would get spiritual brownie points if they helped in studies that protected the purity of these holy works.

Dozens of grammarians worked to bring structure to Sanskrit grammar. You might recognize some of these structures. In the alphabets of most Indian languages that have been derived from Sanskrit, the vowels are grouped together first, and then the consonants. Even the consonants are placed in groups, divided according to which part of the mouth and throat they are pronounced from.

And it worked! Today, the Vedas are chanted in exactly the same way as they were 4000 years ago, with no mistakes, no discrepancies.

The major credit for this goes to Panini. Very little is known about Panini's origins. It is not even known exactly when he lived. But based on what he wrote in his works, researchers have concluded that he lived around the 5th century BCE. It is believed that he was born in Shalatula, near the Indus river in northwestern India, what is now Pakistan. He lived, worked and died in northern India.

Panini built upon the work of all the grammarians and linguists before him. His opus was a work called *Ashtadhyayi*. Ashta means Eight, Adhyaya is Chapter—and the *Ashtadhyayi* contains, well, eight chapters.

Incidentally, the Brahmi script used for Sanskrit didn't come into use until 200-300 years after Panini, so it is not known whether Panini used any other existing script to write it, or whether he just composed it in his head, and relied on his disciples to act as his walking-talking notepads! If it was the latter, then the *Ashtadhyayi* must also have been passed down orally until a suitable script was developed to write it down.

The *Ashtadhyayi* is a complete, concise analysis of the grammatical structure of Sanskrit. It is a very small piece of work. In printed pages, it runs to about forty in number. But if translated into English, it'll take 1300 sheets to print it all out. So essentially, it is a very dense work. The *Ashtadhyayi* has 3976 rules. These rules are, in turn, lists themselves. You can think of it like a secret code, with each letter or alphabet standing for another word or phrase. And each of those words or phrases define another rule. To avoid repetition, some of the rules have been compressed into one single rule.

Complex? It is. Sanskrit is an extremely precise language, and Panini captured the essence of the language. It is almost as if he compressed it and bottled it up, so that it could be passed on easily from person to person.

You could think of the *Ashtadhyayi* as a word-generating device. An algorithm, even. If you input a phoneme or morpheme, it generates words and sentences.

Sounds suspiciously like computer programming? You're right. The *Ashtadhyayi* even uses principles, which we now associate with programming languages.

Units of Language

Phoneme: Distinct and basic unit of sound in a language. For example, in the word 'cat', 'c', 'a' and 't' are the three phonemes.

Morpheme: Smallest grammatical unit of a word that provides a specific meaning to a string of letters. For example, in the word 'unlikely', 'un', 'like' and 'ly' are the morphemes.

It has been compared to a Turing machine: a mathematical model that breaks down the logical structure of any computer device to its essentials. In this case, the *Ashtadhyayi* breaks down speech and language into the basic elements and gives the definition of the function of these elements.

In the 18th and 19th centuries, when Western scientists were trying to find ways to analyze and structure the grammar of Western languages, they discovered Panini's works. They realized that it was as if they were trying to reinvent the wheel. The *Ashtadhyayi* already had all the linguistic principles they were trying to figure out. They based their studies and derived heavily from Panini's work. Linguists like Ferdinand de Saussaure and Noam Chomsky were influenced by his work. Walter Eugene Clark, a philologist (one who studies ancient texts), calls Panini's grammar the earliest scientific grammar in the world, and thought that it revolutionized the study of languages in the West. Even now, linguists borrow theoretical ideas from Panini's work.

And then, computers were invented. Initially, codes and programme for a computer were written using machine-code language and assembly language. But they were full of numbers and symbols and they were hard to understand. As programming became more complicated, it became necessary to develop a computer language that was less like a bunch of numbers, and more like spoken or natural-sounding language, so that it would be easier to use and understand. So they turned to language theory for help, which, of course, was based on Panini's insights and ideas.

If you have heard people say that Sanskrit is the foundation for high-level programming language, this is the reason. And yes, Sanskrit would probably make a great programming language!

Here's something interesting. If you've heard old English, or even English from two centuries ago, you'll know how different it sounds. Sometimes you can't even understand it. Why, I'm sure there are some words you use that your parents can't understand. Language is like that, it changes very quickly, and spoken language comes into the written language almost immediately.

But the thing with written Sanskrit is that it has remained unchanged. If you happen to dig up a letter written in Sanskrit in an archaeological site, unless you perform tests on the paper and ink, you won't know whether it was written ten or thousand years ago!

ashoka

(304–232 BCE)

Who: Indian Emperor

How he changed the world: One of the greatest emperors of the world, probably created the first welfare state. Played a critical role in developing Buddhism into a world religion.

It was the most abrupt and extraordinary U-turn in history. Ashoka, the ruthless and ambitious monarch, was intent upon expanding his empire. He spared nobody, not even his brothers, in his quest to become the supreme ruler of India. And then, almost overnight, he underwent a profound transformation and went down in history as one of the earliest proponents of peace and love.

Ashoka was the grandson of Chandragupta Maurya, the founder of the Maurya dynasty. Ashoka's father was the emperor Bindusara. Ashoka's older brothers were the obvious heirs to the throne. But Ashoka successfully led several military conquests for his father, and became popular across the empire. So he quickly became Bindusara's favourite as his successor. After Bindusara died, Ashoka conducted a prolonged power struggle with his brothers. It ended with Ashoka killing them all, and he ascended the throne in 269 BCE.

He conquered more kingdoms, and extended his empire to cover nearly the whole of present-day India, except for a small region in the extreme south. His influence extended even to Sri Lanka, Afghanistan and beyond.

About eight years after Ashoka became king, he attacked the powerful kingdom of Kalinga (modern-day Odisha and parts of Andhra). Kalinga had a mighty army, but it was no match for Ashoka's formidable military strength. Ashoka routed the Kalinga army and conquered the kingdom. More than 100,000 soldiers are said to have been killed in this terrible battle.

After the battle, Ashoka triumphantly marched into the capital of Kalinga—and came to an abrupt halt. Bodies lay everywhere, and children and women wailed for their loved ones. Buildings lay shattered, in ruins.

Ashoka was overwhelmed with sorrow and regret.

'What have I done?' he lamented. He managed to step back and take a good look at his life and decisions. He questioned his actions. 'What is victory, after all?' he thought. 'What is valour? Is it right to add to my own splendour by destroying the grandeur of another kingdom?'

As Ashoka wrestled with these existential questions, he discovered Buddhism. (According to some historical accounts, he was already familiar with Buddhism before the Kalinga war.) The principles of Buddhism appealed to his troubled mind. He resolved to move away from his bloodthirsty past and lead life according to the Buddhist principles of non-violence and compassion for all life.

Ashoka decided to follow the path of Dhammavijaya—Conquest with Dharma; dharma is a hard-to-translate word, loosely defined in English as righteousness, or the right conduct, and the correct way of life. He swore to dedicate his life to serve his subjects and all humanity, and spread among his people the principles of Buddhism.

Ashoka travelled around his kingdom speaking to his subjects and preaching the message of peace. He tried to persuade people to live honestly and peaceably, lead a simple life and be kind to all living beings. He inscribed edicts on rocks and pillars (known as the pillars of Ashoka) throughout India. These edicts were statements outlining his ideas of the right thoughts and actions of a good citizen. They were based on Buddhist principles.

Ashoka strived to popularize Buddhism, and organized the third international Buddhist council, presided over by the fabulously named Moggaliputta Tissa, Ashoka's spiritual guide. He sent missionaries all across the country and as far as western Asia and into the Greek territories. His children Mahindra and Sanghamitra went to Sri Lanka as missionaries. Though Buddhism didn't catch on in Western regions at that time, it became popular in Sri Lanka, and even now, Sri Lanka has a large Buddhist population.

Within a few centuries, Buddhism was the primary religion in large tracts of Southeast Asia, China, Japan. It is no exaggeration to say that without Ashoka's efforts, Buddhism would probably have died out, and wouldn't have been a world religion.

Ashoka was a progressive ruler. He laid the foundation for one of the first welfare states in the world. (A welfare state is a system where the government undertakes measures to protect the well-being of its citizens, especially those in need.)

He started schools, founded hospitals for both people and animals, and dug wells. He planted trees on the sides of roads, and built free rest houses for travellers. He issued rules against animal sacrifice, and the hunting of animals.

In spite of the scale and grandeur of his rule, the stunning drama of his life, and the astonishing contrasts between the initial and later days of his rule, Ashoka was completely lost in the mists of history. His edicts were destroyed, and all documents relating to him were lost. He remained unknown for centuries. It was only during the 18th and 19th centuries that British historians and archaeologists dug up and pieced together bits and pieces of his life—like a jigsaw. The story of how Ashoka's life was brought back to life rivals the most exciting mystery stories!

And as the picture became clearer, Ashoka regained his rightful place in history, and he became known around the world for the jaw-dropping story of his life.

It is unlikely that you'll find another monarch who gave up conquest and arms at the height of his powers. Besides, even after that, he was able to keep his large empire and his powers intact without any use of military power!

Ashoka is probably the first emperor in history to practice and preach a policy of pacifism (a belief that violence can't be justified under any circumstances). He also preached non-violence, and sent peace missions to other countries, which was virtually unheard of in those times (and probably caused a lot of suspicion and mistrust until the other countries realized that this guy was earnest!)

His efforts at humanitarianism—working towards improving the well-being of humans—and the establishment of a welfare state, as already mentioned, were one of the first of its kind in the world.

Also, Ashoka's religious tolerance was remarkable. Considering the power and reach that he had, and the conviction of his belief in Buddhism, he could have easily forced his religion upon his subjects. He could have made it a state religion. He could have converted his subjects forcefully. He could have caused trouble for people of other religions. Instead, he just chose to spread his ideas and let his subjects choose their own religion. He respected and tolerated other religions. Besides, in his preaching of Buddhism, it was more the moral and ethical principles that he laid emphasis on, and not its more formal side.

His story is also proof of the fact that it is possible to undergo a change in character and morals to an extreme degree, and that a human being is capable of positive transformation. It is an inspirational thought.

Historical Bias?

Some historians say that Ashoka's previous cruelty has been exaggerated by some Buddhist chroniclers in order to show the before-after contrast, and to say that it was because of Buddhism that he became so noble. But even if we account for some exaggeration, the story remains remarkable.

To borrow the words of the British author H.G. Wells: 'In the history of the world there have been thousands of kings and emperors who called themselves "Their Highnesses", "Their Majesties" and "Their Exalted Majesties" and so on. They shone for a brief moment, and as quickly disappeared. But Ashoka shines and shines brightly like a bright star, even unto this day'.

Ashoka's name might not exactly be echoing across the world in the present time, but in India, he has been immortalized. The Ashoka pillar at Sarnath has a Lion Capital, which has been adopted as the National Emblem of India. The wheel at the base of the Capital is known as 'Ashoka Chakra' and this has been placed on the centre of the flag of India, to depict progress.

bhaskara II
(Bhaskaracharya)

(1114–1185)

Who: Mathematician and astronomer.

How he changed the world: Wrote the first mathematical work with a complete and systematic use of the decimal system. Made astronomical observations and worked with mathematical concepts that mathematicians from other parts of the world caught up with only centuries later.

THERE WAS A GOLDEN AGE, A PERIOD OF ABOUT 700 years, between the 5th century CE and 12th century CE, when Indian scientific knowledge was far more advanced than the rest of the world. Indian scholars made enormous strides in the fields of mathematics, astronomy, medicine, chemistry, philosophy, metallurgy and other areas.

In mathematics, several brilliant scholars like Aryabhata, Bhaskara I, Brahmagupta, Varahamihira and other luminaries had already been working on advanced mathematical and astronomical concepts. And then, in the 12th century, there came into the light Bhaskara II, who represents the peak of mathematical knowledge in ancient India.

Bhaskara II is also known as Bhaskaracharya to distinguish him from the other mathematician Bhaskara I, who lived and worked in the 7th century CE. His contributions to the field of astronomy and mathematics have led to him being regarded as the greatest Indian mathematician of all time, and his contribution to world mathematics is significant. His mathematical works used the decimal system, and were one of the first to do so. His understanding of mathematical and astronomical concepts was extremely advanced—the Western world took many more centuries to catch up.

Bhaskaracharya was born near present-day Bijapur in Karnataka. He was the son of a famous astrologer. As a student, he extensively studied mathematics, grammar, medicine, yoga and the vedas, among other subjects. He went on to become the head of the astronomical observatory at Ujjain, the leading centre of mathematical learning in India at that time. Previously, Varahamihira and Brahmagupta had worked there, and they had already built a strong base of study in mathematical astronomy. Bhaskara took over their mantle and continued working in the field, bringing out some of the most memorable and unparalleled works of mathematics and astronomy—the major ones being *Leelavati, Beejaganita* and *Siddhanta Shiromani.*

Leelavati is his most famous work. It sometimes seems to be addressing a woman, giving rise to the legend that he wrote it for his daughter Leelavati. The story goes that Bhaskara predicted the auspicious time for his daughter's wedding. Then, he set up a container full of water, and on it, he placed a small cup with a tiny hole. He told her that the moment at which the cup filled up with water and sank, would be the best time for her to get married. However, Leelavati bent over the container to see how full the cup was, and a pearl from her jewellery fell into the cup and blocked the hole. The cup never sank and Leelavati didn't get married at all. So apparently, Bhaskara thought it would be a good idea to write a book on mathematics to console her!

Leelavati is a book of mathematical problems. Scholars think that Bhaskara probably meant for a student of *Leelavati* to concentrate on the applications of mathematical methods.

Written completely in verse, *Leelavati* displays Bhaskaracharya's mastery in both mathematics as well as poetry. Imagine not only being a whiz at math, but being able to express everything in the form of poetry, complete with perfect metre!

Leelavati includes works based on the studies of Bramhagupta, Sridhara and Padmanabha—other mathematicians before him; but Bhaskara also introduced new topics and systemized the whole study of mathematics. He also introduced new and improved methods to solve problems.

Leelavati brings mathematics to life using everyday examples and scenes from daily life. For instance, in one problem, a woman's necklace snaps, and Bhaskaracharya gives you the fraction of pearls that roll away from her, the fraction that she catches, and so on, and from the number of pearls remaining on the string, the student is expected to calculate how many pearls were on the necklace in the first place.

Then there is a problem that deals with right-angled triangles, which involves a bird sitting on the top of a straight pole, spying a snake in the grass.

Then there's one about Shiva, where Shiva holds different weapons in each of his ten arms, and the question is—how many forms should Shiva take if each time, each hand is to be holding a different object? Yes, this is a problem on permutations, and the answer is 10 factorial!

Similarly, Bhaskaracharya included problems on inverse proportion, arithmetic and geometric progression, and indeterminate equations. He suggested different ways to multiply and square numbers. There are also problems involving interest, and geometry, of course.

Beejaganita is about algebra. Bhaskaracharya used letters to represent numbers. He proposed that minus and minus make plus, and minus and plus make minus. He was also one of the first to realize that a square has a negative as well as a positive square root.

There is an equation, $Nx^2 + 1 = y^2$, which is now called 'Pell's equation'. Bhaskaracharya called it the *varga prakriti* (equation of the multiplied square) and he gave a solution called Chakravala. This is a cyclic method of solving the equation, and it involves only a few easy steps. He gave many solutions to solve this equation, and these solutions have been discussed widely. Never mind if all this seems too much to understand, here's something interesting about this equation. In the 17th century, French mathematician Pierre de Fermat proposed this equation as a mathematical challenge to his friend Frenicle de Bessy, thinking that he was giving his friend a humongous challenge. Little did he know that a mathematician in India had solved it five centuries ago!

Bhaskaracharya was also probably the first to talk about the concept of infinity, and that a number divided by 0 is infinite. He says this with the help of a philosophical metaphor.

'In the numerical quantity that has zero as the denominator, there is no change if anything is added or subtracted. Just as the infinite and immutable lord is unchanged when creatures are absorbed into him at the end of the world, or emerge from him at the creation of the world.'

But scholars say that it is likely that Bhaskaracharya didn't completely understand the concept of infinity.

Bhaskara's contributions were most significant in astronomy. There were other astronomers before him, like Aryabhata, who first proposed that the Earth spun around its axis. But Bhaskara's work was much more extensive and influential.

He wrote *Siddhanta Shiromani*, considered a theoretical work par excellence. It is a very detailed work, with lots of theories, and includes everything there was to know about Indian astronomy and mathematics at that time. For his calculations in this book, he uses concepts in trigonometry and calculus that hadn't ever been used before. His work pre-dates the same work conducted by European mathematics by five or six centuries!

The book had rules for calculating everything you wanted to know about the position of the planets, stars, sun and moon, at any given time. Like his predecessors, Bhaskaracharya was aware of the concept of gravity, and mentions it in the book.

He also calculated accurately the time required for the Earth to orbit around the sun. He discovered that the moon's orbit around the Earth varies regularly due to the sun's attractive forces.

Bhaskara also studied observational astronomy, and in the section 'Yantradhyaya' of the book, he describes a large number of astronomical instruments. In 'Grahaganitam', he computed eclipses and planetary motions. In 'Goladhyaya', he considered the sky as 'a celestial sphere' and wrote down the rules of astronomy.

Bhaskara's works (and Brahmagupta's before him) were translated into Arabic by Arab scholars. The influence of his work can be seen in the work of these Arab mathematicians. Through them, these theories, based on the decimal system, reached Europe, where European mathematicians studied and made further progress in the fields during the Renaissance period.

Bhaskara taught mathematics to his son Lokasamudra who helped establish a school in 1207 dedicated to studying Bhaskara's works. However, it wasn't enough to sustain the study of mathematics, apparently, as Bhaskara was the last spark. After him, Indian science went into a decline for the next 800 years or so.

Before we go, here's a problem from *Leelavati* for you to solve.

On an expedition to seize his enemy's elephants, a king marched two yojanas the first day. Tell me, intelligent calculator, with what increasing rate of daily march did he proceed, since he reached his foe's city, a distance of eighty yojanas, in a week?

(A yojana is a unit of measurement of distance in Vedic times, and 1 yojana was about 12 to 15 kilometres.)

Solution:

This is a problem of arithmetic progression. That is, every following day, the king has to travel a little more than he did the previous day. Let's refer to that factor, or that rate of acceleration, as 'a'.

So, he has to travel 'a' yojanas more than he did the previous day.

So,

A	B
Day	Yojanas travelled
1	2
2	2 + a
3	2 + 2a, which we got from (2+a+a)
4	2 + 3a
5	2 + 4a
6	2 + 5a
7	2 + 6a

Now, the total of the distances in column B is the total distance travelled.

That gives us 14 + 21a.

We already know that this is 80 yojanas.

14+ 21a = 80

Solving, we get, a = 66/21 = 22/7 yojanas.

So, each day, the king has to travel 22/7 yojanas more than the previous day.

The Decline of Science in India

If you're wondering why there was no further advancement in Indian science and mathematics after the 12th century in spite of such a rich and glorious tradition, P.C. Ray, the 19th-century chemist, has an explanation for it. He says that the introduction of the caste system in its strict form prevented the interaction and exchange of ideas between doers and thinkers in society. Besides, the shastras were introduced, which laid down rules about what can or cannot be done (no studying the human body!). Third, the Vedanta philosophy became popular, and it said that the material world was 'maya', or an illusion, and it frowned upon the study of physical science.

tipu sultan

20 November 1750–4 May 1799

Who: 18th-century ruler of Mysore.

How he changed the world: Tipu is known as the father of modern missile technology. The rocket weaponry that Tipu used in warfare against the British was so technically advanced for that age that the British learned it from him and then used them in wars around the world.

5TH APRIL 1799: TIPU SULTAN OF MYSORE HAD already fought three wars against the British in the last couple of decades. Once again, he was holding out against the British army in his island capital of Shrirangapatna. He expected the British to mount an attack from the south. He stationed a regiment of soldiers in a tope (grove) in Sultanpet, a little to the south of Shrirangapatna.

Colonel Wellesley (later a hero at the Battle of Waterloo, and came to be known as the Duke of Wellington) was in charge of the 33rd regiment of the British army. The regiment was charged with clearing out the tope before progressing towards the capital.

After dark, the regiment prepared themselves. All was still. The regiment crept up in the dark, muskets at the ready, and approached the tope.

And suddenly there was chaos: muskets firing; explosions of blue light; loud sounds of shells bursting in the air.

A torrent of rockets pummelled the British army. The British had no idea what hit them. They didn't know from where they were being attacked, and with what. They lost their bearings and couldn't proceed. They retreated in utter disorder. Captain Wellesley flew back to camp, and didn't turn up the next day when a new attack was planned. He finally did emerge later, after he recovered. But according to his biographer, he never quite got over this shock, and even after he retired, he remembered this day with awe.

British historians later wrote about these rocket attacks in great detail, especially the way that they caught the British armies unawares. They attributed these attacks to Tipu Sultan, the ruler of a small kingdom, who managed to create waves all over the Western world with his missile technology.

Tipu Sultan (sometimes spelled Tippu Sultan) was born Fateh Ali Sahab Tipu, in 1750 in Devanahalli. His father Hyder Ali was the ruler of Mysore. Tipu was trained in military tactics by French officers in his father's army. As a commander under his father, he fought against the Marathas for years. He succeeded his father in 1782 and ruled from his capital Shrirangapatna (10 km from present-day Mysore). He waged four wars against the British East

India Company, fighting hard to keep his kingdom from falling into their hands. During the fourth war in 1799, Tipu was killed.

On the one hand, Tipu was an able administrator. He brought in some landmark changes in the administration, introduced new coins, helped in the growth of Mysore's silk industry, and made Mysore a major economic power. On the other hand, he was known for being ruthless, especially towards his enemies, and there are records of his massacres of innocents. Even today, he is steeped in controversy, as some historians paint him as a valiant freedom fighter, tolerant of other religions, while others argue that he was a tyrant who forcibly converted people to Islam.

But what we do know for sure is that he was a technology buff. He liked innovation, and was curious about the latest European inventions and machines. He had laboratories and workshops and encouraged artisans to manufacture all kinds of devices. He liked to experiment with the latest in technology.

Rockets for warfare had already been in use for a long time in south India. A rocket was a term for any missile that whizzed forward when fuel was ejected from its rear end; they worked on Newton's third law of motion, i.e., every action has an equal and opposite reaction. They were very similar to the rockets we use now for fireworks. The only difference is that these rockets were attached to spears or swords. When the rockets were fired, the weapons were propelled forward to cover great distances.

For a long time, the rockets were made of paper and other flimsy material. So these rocket tubes couldn't hold too much gunpowder or other such propellants. Tipu's father Hyder Ali started using iron tubes for these rockets. At that time, the iron available in India, made from traditional technology, was much better in quality than the iron available in the Western world. Using iron for the tubes meant that it could withstand higher pressure. So a large quantity of gunpowder could be packed in tightly. When fired up, the iron tubes withstood the high pressures, and so, the backward thrust was much higher. As a result, the rocket weapons were expelled with tremendous force, and travelled much farther than ever before. In some cases, they covered up to 1 km, which was remarkable for the time.

Traditional Method of Iron-making

Traditionally, iron was made in and around Mysore in small smelting houses. While the iron for household and agricultural implements was made with iron ore mined out of rocks, the iron for weapons was made from a raw material unique to the area: black sand found on riverbeds. During the monsoons, the torrential waters of the rivers would erode the iron ore found in rocks near the mouths of the rivers, creating this black sand. This sand would be available only for four months. It was smelted using charcoal, and made into iron that was impure but malleable, which was perfect for shaping weapons. This same iron was also used to make the world-famous Wootz steel.

Tipu's rockets consisted of these gunpowder-filled iron tubes attached to long spears—bamboo canes with sharp iron tips. These lethal weapons could be set loose upon the enemy from afar. The rockets made loud noises and burst in the air like shells, while the spears rained down on the enemy. There were ground rockets too. These rockets had weights tied to them. So they didn't fly into the air, but moved close to the ground haphazardly in a serpentine manner, injuring soldiers left and right, until the rockets died out.

The rockets were not very accurate, though. If you were aiming at a particular target, you couldn't be sure that your rocket would hit it. However, as a mass attack on a large army, or as a diversionary tactic, it proved effective. Besides, this was an entirely new technology, and these projectile weapons took the enemy by surprise and caused great terror in the ranks.

Hyder Ali and Tipu used these rockets to great effect in the second Anglo–Mysore war at Pollilur in 1780. The British East India Company army hadn't seen anything like it before, and the rockets probably caused more fear than injury, but they worked. Accounts of the fearsome Mysorean rockets reached Britain and Europe.

After Tipu took over the kingdom, he increased

the number of rocket troops in his army from 1200 to 5000 in number. He allocated large areas of land to the manufacture and study of these missiles. He used them again to his advantage in battles against the British in the third Anglo–Mysore war from 1789–92, which, once again, he won.

Tipu used the rockets once again during the fourth Mysore war. However, the rockets couldn't do much for Tipu when, in the final battle of these wars, the British stormed his capital and killed him.

But the rockets had made their mark in history. British officers sent 500 of these rockets to the Royal Woolwich Arsenal in Britain, for the artillery officers there to study. It was then that Sir William Congreve, an English artillery officer and inventor, started experimenting on his own rockets, based on these Mysorean rockets. He increased their range, and improved their accuracy. These came to be known as Congreve rockets.

The British used Congreve rockets in wars throughout Europe, including in wars against Napoleon. These rockets were even used in the British attack on Fort McHenry, near Baltimore,

Maryland in the US in 1814. The poet Francis Scott Key, who watched the battle from afar, was awed by the explosions and ballistics, and wrote a poem where he spoke about 'The rockets' red glare', referring to these Congreve rockets. That poem, known as 'The Star-Spangled Banner', is now the national anthem of the US!

rabindranath tagore

7 May 1861–7 August 1941

Who: Poet, novelist, playwright, composer, artist, Nobel Laureate

How he changed the world: The first global literary star in history. The Universal Man, a symbol of Indian culture, who tried to combine the best of the East and the West. Influenced poets, writers, artists and lay people in India and all over the world.

DURING WORLD WAR I, THE GURKHA REGIMENT OF the British Army was fighting in Germany. An Indian soldier from the regiment was badly wounded in both legs, taken prisoner and brought to the hospital at the front. The German chief surgeon knew he would have to amputate the soldier's legs in order to save his life, and tried to communicate this to the wounded soldier. But the soldier was out of his wits with pain and terror. He was thrashing about, not listening to what the doctor was trying to convey. Besides, neither knew the other's language. Time was running out. Then, the assistant surgeon, who was standing by, hit upon an idea. He bent close to the Indian soldier and whispered to him the only Indian name he knew. 'Rabindranath Tagore! Rabindranath Tagore!' he said. The soldier immediately relaxed, smiled softly and let the doctors work on him.

This incident was narrated by Carl Zuckmayer, a German playwright, who was friends with the assistant surgeon in the story. Neither the assistant surgeon, says Zuckmayer, nor the soldier likely knew anything about Tagore apart from his name. And yet, that name carried enough weight to sow the seed of goodwill across cultures!

That was the kind of influence Rabindranath Tagore, one of the first global men of the 20th century, wielded on the world.

Rabindranath Tagore was born in a scholarly and influential family. His grandfather was one of the richest men in Calcutta, with investments in banking and mining, and with connections to the East India Company. His father, a religious reformer, was an influential leader of the Brahmo Samaj—a society that aimed to reform Hinduism and the Hindu way of life. Tagore grew up in a household that was the centre of a kind of renaissance in Bengal, brimming with new ideas and action, and frequently visited by distinguished people.

Tagore started writing at an early age, and published his first book of poems at the age of sixteen, under the pseudonym Bhanu Singh Thakur. In his late teens, he went to England to study law at University College, London, but he didn't finish his degree. He came back to India and continued publishing stories, novels and poetry that became popular throughout Bengal.

When he was twenty-nine, Tagore started managing the family's ancestral estates at Shilaidaha. He was troubled by the problems of the poor villagers under his charge, and tried to improve their lives. He was also deeply affected by the beauty and solitude of that place. He wrote dozens of stories during this time, which made up his first collection of short stories.

A few years later, Tagore founded an experimental school in Shantiniketan, based on the ancient gurukul system. Meanwhile, he became a strong supporter of the struggle for Indian Independence, and got involved in the Swadeshi movement.

In 1910, Tagore wrote the *Gitanjali*, a collection of poems. He translated the poems into English, and two years later, he went to England with the English manuscript to meet the artist William Rothenstein.

Rothenstein had met Tagore earlier in Calcutta, and made sketches of him. He had been impressed by Tagore's 'inner charm'. Rothenstein was one of the people who set up the India Society in London to widen public understanding of Indian art and culture, so Tagore wanted to give him the manuscript of *Gitanjali.* On the way to meet Rothenstein, disaster nearly struck. Tagore, awed and distracted by the sights of London, forgot the manuscript in the London tube! Thankfully, he found it later in the office of lost property. He would look back on this incident from time to time and shudder at what would have happened if he'd lost the manuscript!

Rothenstein loved *Gitanjali*, and showed it to the poet William Butler Yeats. Yeats read it, and was immediately charmed by it. To him, Tagore represented the wisdom and dignity of the East. The poems proved to Yeats that Asian philosophy was as strong and vibrant as he had always believed. Yeats became Tagore's greatest advocate. Yeats said that he sometimes had to put the collection away and not read it in public, because he didn't want people to see how moved he was by it.

Yeats wrote the introduction to *Gitanjali*, and it was published by the India Society. Later, the book was reprinted by Macmillan. Gradually, several other poets in England, including Robert Frost and Robert

Bridges, became Tagore's admirers. Ezra Pound got Tagore's poems published in America. When the poet Wilfred Owen died in World War I, he had a book in his pocket inscribed by lines from Tagore's poetry.

Tagore's fame spread across Europe and the US. He looked exactly like the picture that the West had of a mystic wise man from the East—a striking figure, with flowing robes, a long beard and soulful eyes. He was even referred to as 'The Sage from the Orient'. This image propelled his popularity, as did the content of his poetry, which held gems of wisdom and universal human truths. The Western world was on the brink of the world war, and needed soothing words of wisdom—and they found in his poetry what they were looking for. Tagore came to be known as the Universal Man, the voice of India and a living symbol of India's culture.

In 1913, Tagore was awarded the Nobel Prize in Literature. He was the first non-European to receive the award, nudging out several illustrious writers for the honour.

Tagore travelled to more than thirty countries

across the world, and became the world's first intercontinental literary star. He took the opportunity to speak out about India's spiritual heritage, his educational philosophy, his opinion on war, and much more. Everywhere, he was received with adulation and admiration. Halls were packed wherever he spoke.

The *Gitanjali* was translated into several languages and in many countries, millions of copies were sold.

Tagore's Creative Output

Tagore's creative genius is jaw-dropping—he has written nearly 1000 poems, two dozen plays, eight novels, eight collections of short stories, more than 2200 songs, for which he composed both the music and the lyrics, and a ton of prose on social, political, and other topics. Apart from that, there are his paintings, English translations, and his work as an educator, social reformer and a freedom fighter.

In England, for instance, there were ten reprints of *Gitanjali* even before the Nobel Prize was announced.

Tagore influenced people and poets from various nationalities. His plays were performed in London. He was extremely popular in Japan, and in Russia, his books were translated into Russian and the copies flew off the shelves. He played a major role in Indo–Korean ties, and one of his poems, in which he refers to Korea as the Lamp of the East, is still taught in Korean schools.

The Chilean poet-diplomat and Nobel Laureate Pablo Neruda was deeply impressed with Tagore's work, and wrote several poems that were based on Tagore's poems. Another Nobel Laureate, Juan Ramon Jimenez, translated several works of Tagore into Spanish, and these translations became popular in Spain. The Japanese writer and Nobel Laureate Yasunari Kawabata recalled attending Tagore's lecture as a teenager and being awed by his appearance. Kawabata even referred to and used Tagore's ideas, especially about Japan, in his work.

Tagore enjoyed correspondence with Albert Einstein, H.G. Wells, George Bernard Shaw, Thomas

Mann, Robert Frost and Romain Rolland. He was knighted by King George VI in 1915, but he returned his knighthood in 1919 in protest against the Jallianwala Bagh massacre.

Tagore became closely associated with Gandhi and others of the freedom movement, and though he and Gandhi had different opinions on various issues, they admired each other. Tagore was the one who gave Gandhi the moniker 'Mahatma' while Gandhi referred to him as 'Gurudev'.

In 1921, Tagore started the Vishwabharati University at Shantiniketan, funded by the money he earned from his speaking tours. His vision was a centre of learning that combined the best of both the East and the West.

Tagore spent his later years writing, and started painting as well. He put most of the songs he had written to music, and they are still sung extensively, and are known as Rabindra Sangeet. Two of his songs were adapted as national anthems: 'Jana Gana Mana' of India, and 'Amar Shonar Bangla' of Bangladesh. He is the only person in the world to have written the national anthems of two countries.

Tagore died in 1941 after a long illness. His unbelievable popularity faded very quickly in the West, but he is still revered by millions in India and Bangladesh. His is a towering presence in Indian literature. He made Bangla more contemporary, and changed the face of Bangla literature.

He is still remembered across the world, in the places he visited. His busts stand in some of the most remote places on earth, in places like Cuba, Canada, Fiji, Mexico, US, France, Russia, Germany, and one in Shakespeare's house in England. Some of his works have been made into beautiful award-winning movies by master film-maker Satyajit Ray.

mohandas karamchand gandhi

(2 October 1869–30 January 1948)

Who: Political leader and social activist who led India to freedom from British colonial rule through peaceful and non-violent means.

How he changed the world: Mahatma Gandhi's beliefs and his strategies of non-violent transformation have influenced leaders and activists worldwide, and inspired millions. His is one of the most universally recognized names on earth.

BARACK OBAMA. MARTIN LUTHER KING JR. NELSON Mandela. Albert Einstein. John Lennon. Steve Jobs. The Dalai Lama. Cesar Chavez.

What do all these people have in common?

Each one of them credits Mahatma Gandhi as an inspiration for the work they did. As Barack Obama says, Gandhi inspired him to spread the message that each one of us can be the change that we seek in this world. A portrait of Gandhi hung in his presidential office, to remind him, he says, 'that ordinary people can do extraordinary things'.

And a more ordinary boy than young Mohandas you wouldn't find. Extremely shy and physically weak, he was an average student. (One report said that he was 'good at English, fair in Arithmetic and weak in Geography; conduct very good, bad handwriting.') He was so troubled by fear of the dark that he slept with the lights on at night. The story of how this unremarkable child went on to become one of the most influential figures in the history of the world is nothing short of extraordinary.

Mohandas Karamchand Gandhi was born on

2 October 1869 in Porbandar, Gujarat. Mohandas was a diligent and truth-loving boy, who was deeply influenced by and attached to his mother who was a very religious person. The teenaged Mohandas wanted to study medicine, but his family advised him to study law, as it would give him a better chance of landing a good job. He relented. (It would be an interesting exercise to discuss how different India would have been had he become a doctor!)

So, when he was nineteen, he set sail to London to study law. He struggled to adapt to Western clothing, etiquette and food. Vegetarianism in fact was a struggle, and an embarrassment to him until he came upon a book defending vegetarianism. He joined the London Vegetarian Society, and found a voice for his convictions. During this time, he met men and women who believed in universal brotherhood and introduced him to the Bible and the *Bhagavad Gita*. The *Gita* would become the greatest source of inspiration in his life.

He came back to India with a degree, but he had difficulty being a lawyer. He was terrified of public speaking (would you believe it?) and fled the courtroom during his first court case, attacked by a bout of nervousness.

He didn't find any other jobs, until, when he was twenty-four, he sailed to South Africa to assist an Indian firm in a legal case. He was supposed to stay there for just a year, but ended up staying for twenty years. It was here that he was transformed into the leader that the world is familiar with. But what happened, exactly?

He saw that Indians experienced racial discrimination in South Africa. They could hold only menial jobs, couldn't go out without special permits and were taxed heavily. He himself had several unpleasant experiences. But there was one incident that affected him the most. He was travelling first class on train with a valid ticket. But his white co-passengers complained about a 'coloured' person travelling with them. Gandhi was asked to leave the first-class compartment, but he refused. So, Gandhi was thrown out of the train at Pietermaritzburg station, leaving him confused and distressed. This was the day that the seed of non-violent action was planted in his head.

When Gandhi's work contract in South Africa came to an end, his friends arranged a farewell party for him. At the gathering, someone told him that a bill was being passed by South Africa to deprive Indians of the right to vote. Gandhi couldn't take it lying down. Overnight, he turned into a political campaigner. He organized protests through petitions and press propaganda, and united the Indians in South Africa. He also made their condition known back in India. Though he couldn't prevent the bill from being passed, he gave Indians a voice and brought international recognition to the situation.

His friends and acquaintances persuaded him to stay back, practice law in South Africa and organize the Indian community. He agreed and stayed on. Among other things, he launched Satyagraha, the first mass civil-disobedience movement against the government's restrictions on Hindu marriages, inspiring Indians to protest peacefully. Under his leadership, thousands of Indians sacrificed their livelihood and courted arrests to fight for dignity. Finally, the government buckled, abolished tax and legalized Hindu marriages.

Finally, when he left South Africa, the South African statesman Jan Christian Smuts said, in enormous relief, 'The saint has left our shores—I hope forever.'

When Gandhi, a changed man, came back to India, he found that it had awakened, and was deep in the independence movement, very different from when he left it.

Two major events occurred in 1919. The Rowlatt Act was passed, authorizing the British to imprison suspects without trial. The unfairness of it made Gandhi plunge into the Indian freedom struggle. And then there was the terrible Jallianwala Bagh massacre in Punjab: troops of the British Indian army fired at Indian protesters who had gathered in an enclosed space, killing hundreds, and injuring many more. Gandhi was shocked, and in protest, he returned the Queen's South Africa campaign medal he had received for military service in South Africa. (What? Military service, and that too, in the British army? Yes! During the Second Boer War and the Zulu War in South Africa, Gandhi had raised an

Indian ambulance corps in which he had served as a Sergeant Major for the British army).

Gandhi launched the Satyagraha movement in India. This made him famous on the national stage as millions of Indians responded to his call. He also called for the non-cooperation movement, urging Indians to boycott foreign goods and institutions. Thousands of Indians participated, getting themselves willingly arrested in the process. Gandhi also converted the Indian National Congress from an elite group into an organization of the common people.

Gandhi led the Salt Satyagraha, or Dandi March, in 1930, in protest against the government's tax on salt, which affected even the poorest sections of society. It was the most successful of his non-violent campaigns.

In 1934, Gandhi took a backseat from politics and worked on building India. He wore only Indian clothes, and travelled extensively across India, choosing to travel in third-class compartments of the trains with poor Indians. He participated in protests by mill owners and workers, and helped them fight for their rights. He strived to educate rural India, encouraging local handicrafts and cottage industries. He evolved a system of education suited to Indians. He worked to fight untouchability, and tried to strengthen communal ties. His two ashrams, Sabarmati and Sevagram, were centres of his social and political work in India. He wrote several letters, articles and books, including his autobiography, *The Story of My Experiments with Truth*.

India wanted self-governance, and in 1942, Stafford Cripps came to India with a proposal that India should support Britain during World War II and in exchange, they would give India self-governance after the War. The deal didn't work, because Britain only promised self-governance in the uncertain future, and not immediately. Besides, the British tried to promote discord among Hindus and Muslims. Disappointed with these developments, and spurred on by other factors, Gandhi called for the British to leave India immediately—a campaign known as the Quit India Movement.

In 1945, the Labour Party won in Britain, and finally, Britain began negotiating with the Indian

National Congress and the Muslim League for India's freedom. Gandhi hoped for a unified India, but to his disappointment, the subcontinent was divided into India and Pakistan along religious lines. Violence broke out and Gandhi's appeals to keep the peace went unheard, even as India won Independence in 1947.

In 1948, Gandhi was shot dead by Nathuram Godse, who felt that Gandhi appeased Muslims at the cost of Hindu interests.

Gandhi went down in history as probably the greatest apostle of peace. Even the British, with whom he was constantly at odds, viewed him with admiration and awe.

He had a lot of critics, unhappy with his ideas and actions. Some thought he was too soft, some complained that he wasn't serious about evicting the British. His work as a social reformer wasn't welcomed too warmly by the Dalit community, who felt he was being condescending towards them. Hindus thought he was too soft towards Muslims, and Muslims thought he was partial to his own religion.

But still, his fame has spread wide, and as the decades have gone by, people across India and the world continue to be awed and inspired by how a single person took on entire empires and brought about so much change in the world.

India calls him the Father of the Nation, and every major city in India has a Mahatma Gandhi Road, as do many cities across the world. More than seventy countries have installed statues of Gandhi, and many countries have also issued postage stamps honouring him.

Some of the greatest leaders of the world have looked to him for inspiration, and he has been the guide for several major revolutions in the world.

Martin Luther King Jr, the leader of the Civil Rights Movement in the US, tried to bring social and legal equality to African Americans in the US. He turned to the teachings and methods of Gandhi for inspiration, and even made a journey to India to learn more about Gandhi. He said that he was convinced that 'non-violent resistance is the most potent weapon available to oppressed people in their struggle for freedom.' He referred to Gandhi's teachings as his ‘guiding light’. He said that in his work, ‘Christ gave us the goals, and Mahatma Gandhi the tactics.’

Nelson Mandela, the first black president of South Africa, fought apartheid in his country. He followed Gandhi’s methods of non-violent civil disobedience and urged everybody to pay heed to the lessons of Mahatma Gandhi.

Gandhi also inspired Aung San Suu Kyi, the resistance leader from Myanmar, and Cesar Chavez,

The Gandhi Club

Though Gandhi himself was never given the Nobel Peace Prize—an omission that the Nobel committee has regretted—there is a little Gandhi-club right inside the Nobel Peace Prize winners’ list: Martin Luther King Jr, Nelson Mandela, Aung San Suu Kyi, Barack Obama and The Dalai Lama have all been followers of Gandhian principles!

the American labour leader and civil rights activist who worked for the rights of farmers.

The Dalai Lama calls himself a follower of Gandhi, saying that he has been a source of inspiration ever since he was a small boy growing up in Tibet.

John Lennon said that Gandhi influenced his music, and his views on peace. Al Gore, Will Durant, Ho Chi Minh, U Thant, Steve Jobs, Richard Attenborough, and writers like George Bernard Shaw and Pearl S. Buck were influenced by him.

Albert Einstein was a great admirer of Gandhi, and they wrote to each other regularly. He said, 'Generations to come will scarcely believe that such a man walked upon this earth.'

swami vivekananda

12 January 1863–4 July 1902

Who: A Hindu monk

How he changed the world: Introduced Hinduism, Yoga, and the Indian philosophy of Vedanta to the West. Raised interfaith awareness, established Hinduism as a major world religion. Known as the Ambassador of Hinduism to the United States.

IN 1893, A VERY UNUSUAL CONFERENCE WAS HELD IN Chicago, US. Leaders from all faiths and religions had travelled long distances from around the globe, and had gathered at the World's Parliament of Religions, in an attempt to have a global discussion on faiths.

A hush fell upon the gathering as Swami Vivekananda, a young monk in a turban and flowing robes, stepped up to the podium. 'Sisters and brothers of America'*—he began, and his words were drowned in a standing ovation that lasted for minutes. Whether his appearance overwhelmed the audience, or whether the unique greeting floored them is not entirely clear. Once the applause faded, the thirty-year-old man, with the 'strong and intelligent face', as per press reports, continued to speak, his 'earnest words and the rich, rhythmical utterance' mesmerizing the audience—and creating history. Swami Vivekananda's speeches at this Parliament and after, have been credited for

---

* Some sources say that this is apocryphal—that Vivekananda didn't greet his audience this way at all. There is not enough proof either way. But this is the largely accepted version of events.

introducing Hinduism, yoga, Eastern philosophy and spirituality to the West.

Swami Vivekananda was born Narendranath Datta, on 12 January 1863 in Kolkata, to affluent parents. His father, an attorney in the High Court, had a progressive, rational attitude, whereas his mother was a devout person. The combination of these two influences probably shaped Naren's attitudes very early on.

Naren was quite the Wonderkid. He excelled in academics and music, exercised regularly and played sports. He read widely on philosophy, religion, art and literature. Even during his student days, he was full of curiosity about philosophy, always asking questions about faith and the meaning of life. Wandering ascetics and monks fascinated him. He studied both Indian and Western philosophy, and practiced meditation regularly. When he graduated from Calcutta University with a Bachelor of Arts degree in 1884, the principal of the institution described him as a genius.

Naren was involved with the Brahmo Samaj (a movement that wanted to reform Hinduism) for a while, and was influenced by their ideas of belief in a single god, and denouncing idol-worship. But Naren was restless. He had questions for which he had no answers. He asked several people whether they had come face to face with god, but he wasn't satisfied with the replies he got. Finally, Naren met the spiritual leader Ramakrishna Paramahamsa in the Kali temple at Dakshineshwar, who said, 'Yes, I see Him as I see you, only in a more intense sense.'

Naren was impressed, but he still rebelled against Ramakrishna's spiritual ideas. However around this time, Naren's father died, leaving the family penniless, and Naren found solace in Ramakrishna, finally becoming his disciple. One of the main things he learnt from Ramakrishna was that all living beings are divine; and so, serving mankind is the same as serving God. This principle was to remain with him throughout his life and it influenced all his actions.

After Ramakrishna Paramahamsa died, Naren and the other disciples of Ramakrishna formed a monastic order and took formal vows of sanyaas, renunciation.

Naren then set out to travel across India. He wandered as a monk, with only a staff, a begging bowl, a water container and two books—the *Gita* and *The Imitation of Christ*. During his travels, he interacted with scores of people. The poverty and backwardness that he saw disturbed him, and he vowed to spread education and uplift the masses.

Naren visited Ajit Singh, the ruler of Khetri in Rajasthan. Ajit Singh encouraged him to go to Chicago to attend the Parliament of World Religions. The idea appealed to Naren. He could spread the message of Hinduism, and he could try and get financial help for his idea of improving the conditions of the poor in India. He meditated on what is now known as the Vivekananda rock in Kanyakumari, reflecting on this decision. There, he got what he considered divine permission to undertake this mission. He collected some money from his disciples, and also received funds from Ajit Singh for his travel. In all likelihood, Ajit Singh was the one who taught him to tie a turban in the Rajasthani style—the kind of turban that he is wearing in most of the photographs familiar to us.

It is also widely believed that it was Ajit Singh who asked him to assume the name Swami Vivekananda.

Swami Vivekananda first visited Japan, China and Canada, and then reached Chicago. But there he ran into another obstacle. He found it wasn't going to be as easy to attend the Parliament as he had thought. He would need credentials from a bonafide organization in order for him to participate. But he wasn't part of any such recognized organization—so who would provide him with the required proof of identity? Besides, even if he wanted to attend as a spectator, he would have to wait for some more days until the Parliament opened.

But Vivekananda had very little money. He knew he wouldn't be able to afford the daily expenses for so many extra days. Then, he heard that the living expenses in Boston were lesser than in Chicago, so he went to Boston. There, he met John Henry Wright, a Greek professor in Harvard University, who was deeply impressed with Vivekananda. The professor was horrified to hear why Vivekananda wouldn't be able to attend the Parliament. 'Asking you for credentials is like questioning the sun for its right to shine,' he said. Both he, and a Brahmo Samaj representative who was a member of the Parliament selection committee, ensured that Vivekananda could participate in the Parliament.

And the result, of course, was historic. In his speeches at the Parliament, Vivekananda said that he was proud to belong to a faith that emphasized tolerance and accepted that all religions were true. The audiences liked his idea that we are all one and that there is a universal truth among all faiths. According to his concept of the 'potential divinity of the soul', god is inside every human being, and this 'divine spark' can be cultivated by anybody. This also implied that nobleness is a quality that exists in everybody. This idea appealed to all.

Overnight, he became a sensation in the US. The media referred to him as an 'orator by divine right' and a 'Messenger of Indian Wisdom to the entire world'.

Vivekananda later travelled across the US for years, putting forth in simple words his ideas of religion and philosophy. He built a bridge between Indian and Western culture. He was able to interpret Hindu philosophy in ways that the West could understand and appreciate. He conveyed to them that there is much to learn from Indian philosophy and spiritualism and that it is good for their well-being. He convinced them that India has the potential to contribute to the culture of the world. Vivekananda was the one who introduced

Vedanta Philosophy

Vedanta or Veda+anta means the conclusion of the Vedas, and applies to the Upanishads. So, the school of philosophy that arose from the study of the Upanishads is called Vedanta philosophy. There are several schools of Vedanta philosophy, but in essence, Vedanta believes in the oneness of existence, universal love and harmony, and that the soul is divine. It offers several paths towards understanding our divine nature.

yoga to the US and organized the first few free yoga classes—the popularity of yoga in the US now rivals that of India! He founded centres of Vedanta, a school of Hindu philosophy. He was even offered academic positions at universities, but he refused to accept them as they were against his principles of monkhood.

Vivekananda returned to India in 1897 and toured India, giving lectures. He wanted to raise awareness and knowledge in people and instil in them a pride in their culture. He wanted to unify Hinduism by eradicating sects and castes, and direct the attention of educated people to the condition of the poor.

Swami Vivekananda founded the Ramakrishna Mission. Even today, the mission has centres all over India, and is involved in social service, including running hospitals and educational institutions. It also works in rural development and rehabilitation of the poor.

But all this frenzied activity was taking a toll on his health. In spite of it, he travelled to the US again and then to Europe, before coming back to India and settling at Belur Math near Kolkata.

But his health did not improve. He had asthma, diabetes and insomnia. On 4 July 1902, he retired to his room to meditate, and died. He was only thirty-nine.

Gandhi, Tagore, Nehru, C. Rajaji, and several other famous personalities admired Swami Vivekananda. Jawaharlal Nehru wrote about him: 'Rooted in the past, full of pride in India's prestige, Vivekananda was yet modern in his approach to life's problems, and was a kind of bridge between the past of India and her present.' Rabindranath Tagore told the writer Romain Rolland, 'If you want to know India, study Vivekananda.'

Swami Vivekananda directly or indirectly influenced several people to do good, and work for the improvement of society. For instance, a chance conversation, during a sea voyage, between Jamshedji Tata and Vivekananda influenced the establishment of the world-famous Indian Institute of Science in Bangalore.

Across the world, Mark Twain, Leo Tolstoy, Max Mueller, Lord Kelvin, Gertrude Stein, Aldous Huxley, Nikola Tesla, J.D. Salinger, Lord Kelvin and several other luminaries have been guided by the words of Swami Vivekananda. Many of them met him, attended his lectures, and came away impressed. The French author Romain Rolland wrote one of the first biographies of Swami Vivekananda, and spoke of his 'kingliness' and that he was 'energy personified' and that his 'words are great music'. Authors like Will Durant and Christopher Isherwood wrote about his words and his work.

Sukarno, the former president of Indonesia, was affected by how Swami Vivekananda walked from village to village in India in an effort to regenerate the country. Some of Vivekananda's words—'Don't make your head a library. Put your knowledge into action'—among others, inspired him to fight for the independence of his country from the Dutch.

It is also believed that John D. Rockefeller, the noted philanthropist, made his first substantial philanthropic donation after a conversation with Vivekananda.

How's that for influence!

Vivekananda's lectures have been collected in the form of books that inspire youth even today. His birthday is celebrated as National Youth Day in India. He is frequently quoted in educational institutions across the country to inspire young people. One of his popular quotes is—'Arise, Awake, stop not till the goal is reached.' Perhaps nobody else embodied this quote as much as Swami Vivekananda himself!

c.v. raman

7 November 1888–21 November 1970

Who: Scientist, Nobel Laureate

How he changed the world: Discovered the Raman Effect and Raman spectrography, used all around the world for various applications.

HERE'S A LITTLE GAME FOR YOU. ASK THE PEOPLE around you to name one famous Indian scientist. Go on, I'll wait. Done? Did most of them—if not all—say C.V. Raman? There you go.

And for good reason. After the glorious age of ancient India's supremacy in science and math, there was a lull for centuries until C.V. Raman put India on the global science map again. He was also the second Indian (after Rabindranath Tagore) to get a Nobel Prize, and he was also the first Asian and non-white person to get the Nobel Prize in Physics.

Another remarkable thing about Raman's research is that, contrary to most of the Indian Nobel laureates in science who came after him, his Nobel-winning research work was conducted entirely in India. And that too, when India was still under British rule, and the circumstances weren't too friendly for Indians to excel in their fields.

So, who was this man, and what did he discover?

Chandrasekhara Venkataraman was born in 1888 in Tiruchirappalli, Tamil Nadu. His father was a lecturer in mathematics and physics. Raman's abilities were apparent at an early age. Not only was he a good student, but he was also extremely curious about the world around him. He read advanced textbooks that his father brought home. Raman finished matriculation (the tenth standard) at age eleven. And when he was fifteen, an age where most of us would be writing our tenth standard exams, he finished his BA from Presidency College, Madras, with a gold medal in physics.

Raman's professors encouraged him to go to the UK to do his master's degree. But Raman's doctor didn't like the idea. He said that Raman wasn't healthy enough to endure the severe British climate, and that he should stay back in India. So Raman remained in Presidency College to do his MA. He conducted his own experiments in the labs, and wrote his first paper on the behaviour of light, for *Philosophical Magazine*. After he wrote and published his second paper, he received a letter of appreciation from the distinguished British scientist Lord Rayleigh. The scientist had addressed the letter to 'Professor Raman', not imagining that Raman was just a teenaged student!

When Raman was nineteen, he graduated with top honours in MA. He would have liked to take up a career in science. But his family was poor and in debt, so, Raman joined the highly paid Financial Civil Services as an assistant accountant general. He was posted in Calcutta.

But Raman couldn't let go of science. Every day, after he finished his day job, Raman conducted research at the Indian Association for the Cultivation of Science (IACS) in Calcutta. For over ten years, he mostly worked alone. He was particularly interested in the theory of vibrations, and he experimented with musical instruments such as the violin, veena and tambura, and percussion instruments such as the tabla and mridangam. He used fine chalk powder to observe the vibrational patterns of percussion instruments, and photographed the results. During this time, he wrote and published twenty-seven research papers. He even received research prizes in 1912 and 1913—all this when he was still in a demanding full-time civil services job!

At some point, he started living right next to IACS, to cut down on commute. Not just that, he got a door built that led right from his house into the institute!

He held lectures in popular science at IACS that people flocked to listen to—his live demonstrations, his humour and impressive voice made these lectures all the more attractive.

When he was twenty-nine, Calcutta University offered him the Palit Chair Professorship that had been recently established through an endowment. He resigned from the civil services and he took up this job, even though he knew he would be paid much less than he was in his previous job. But he could now devote more time to science. He continued to lecture and do research, and was well-known as an inspiring lecturer.

He visited England for the first time in 1921, representing Calcutta University in the International Congress of Universities. By that time, he was already a physicist of note, especially in the field of optics (the study of sight and light) and acoustics (the study of sound). He was received warmly in England by eminent scientists J.J. Thompson and Lord Rutherford.

It was on the voyage back to Bombay, on the ship SS Narkunda, that Raman's restless, inquisitive mind started thinking of the question that would change history. He looked out at the beautiful opalescent blue of the Mediterranean Sea, and thought, why is the sea blue?

Lord Rayleigh (the same person who had thought Raman was a professor) had already explained why the sky is blue. You know that sunlight is white and made up of seven colours. If the earth had no atmosphere, then, if you looked up, you would have seen a white sun in a black sky. But the earth does have an atmosphere, and there are gases in it. When sunlight strikes these gas molecules, the colours in it are scattered. Blue light is scattered most, and so we see this light all over the sky, which is why the sky appears blue. Yellow and red light is scattered least, which is why the sun appears yellow, and sometimes red.

Lord Rayleigh said that the sea is blue simply because it reflects the colour of the sky.

But Raman didn't think so. With the help of some simple apparatus that he had in his pocket, he conducted experiments on board the ship, and concluded that the sea was scattering light too. Raman was so charged with excitement that he wrote down his observations while still on the ship, and the moment the ship docked at Bombay, he shot off a letter to the science publication *Nature*, with his observations. Raman was so fired up that he didn't even wait until he got home—the letter carried the postmark of the Bombay harbour!

He went back to Calcutta, and he and his research group started studying the effects of scattering on liquids as well as solids. They passed violet light through a liquid sample. Most of the light that emerged from the liquid sample was violet, but there was also a weak green light along with it. This meant that some of the light particles (photons) scattered by the liquid molecules, underwent a change in wavelength. He also found that the scattering was different through different substances. He made further measurements with more sophisticated instruments, and Raman and his colleague K.S. Krishnan published the results in *Nature* in March 1928. He followed it up with a publication in the

Indian Journal of Physics (which Raman had started) and with a lecture in Bangalore to the South Indian Science Association.

His discovery was called the Raman Effect. It immediately caused waves in the scientific community. It launched more than 700 scientific papers across the world. But why was it so important?

First of all, it was one of the most convincing proofs of the quantum theory (of the atom) because the explanation for the Raman Effect involved the use of photons, atoms, change in energy, and so on.

Second, the Raman Effect was very important because the nature of the scattered radiation depended on the structure of the scattering substance. This meant it could be used to study the characteristics of substances without having to touch or disturb or destroy it. So, even in a mixed sample, you can find out what substance is present, and how much of a substance is present. And it works not only on liquids, but on solids and gases as well!

Raman spectroscopy (the study of the relation between matter and radiation) has now improved tremendously with more and more discoveries and technology. Some examples of its uses: police can use it to analyze drugs at a crime scene without disturbing the evidence. Scientists can analyze nuclear waste from a safe distance. It can be used to identify minerals. It can also give researchers biochemical information that can help in early detection of cancers or other diseases.

Separating Science from the Government

When Raman founded the Raman Research Institute in 1948, the government offered him generous funding. But he refused saying: 'I strongly believe that fundamental science cannot be driven by instructional, industrial and government or military pressures. This was the reason why I decided, as far as possible, not to accept money from the government.'

Raman was awarded the Nobel Prize in Physics in 1930 for this discovery. He was so sure he would get the prize that he had booked tickets to Stockholm even before the award was announced! And until the award was announced, he would pick up the paper each day and scan it urgently for news on the prize, and toss it aside with annoyance when he saw there was no news.

He became the head of the Indian Institute of Science in Bangalore, and later, he started the Indian Academy of Science. He founded and directed the Raman Research Institute in Bangalore, where he remained active in research in various fields and teaching until he died of heart disease in 1970.

Among various other awards and recognition, he was elected a Fellow of the Royal Society, knighted by the British Government, and was awarded the Bharat Ratna by the Indian Government.

In his honour, the Indian government observes National Science Day on his birthday, 28 February, every year.

jawaharlal nehru

14 November 1889–27 May 1964

Who: First prime minister of India

How he changed the world: Architect of modern India. Influenced and led foreign policy that put India on the global stage. Laid the foundation for India's technological and educational advancements.

YOU HAVE READ IN YOUR TEXTBOOKS THAT HE WAS the first prime minister of India. You might have also heard that he had a lot of affection for children, and launched social and educational programmes for their welfare, because of which India celebrates his birthday as Children's Day. But what else do you know about Jawaharlal Nehru?

Jawaharlal Nehru was born in 1889. His father Motilal Nehru was a wealthy lawyer, who also served twice as the president of the Indian National Congress during the Indian independence struggle. Jawaharlal had a privileged childhood. He was privately tutored at home when he was a child. Later, he attended Harrow, a prestigious school in England. He studied natural science in Trinity College, Cambridge, and after that, qualified as a barrister from Inner Temple, London. He came back to India and enrolled himself in the Allahabad High Court, but he found legal practice utterly boring.

Nehru had always yearned for the freedom of his country, but didn't really have ideas on how to go about it, until he met Mahatma Gandhi. Nehru was impressed and influenced by Gandhi's insistence on action, and his ideas about resisting the British without fear or hate. He plunged wholeheartedly into the freedom struggle, and was jailed several times, spending a total of nine years in jail over the next twenty-four years. He used his time in jail to read, study and write several books, including his autobiography, letters to his daughter Indira (who later became the prime minister of India) and *The Discovery of India,* about the heritage, history and philosophy of India.

By the time he was forty, Nehru was popular as the leader of the youth and intellectuals of the country. He became the president of the Indian National Congress, and led the freedom struggle. At the end of World War II, he played a major role in the negotiations leading to India's independence.

India became independent on 15 August 1947, and Nehru took office as the first prime minister of India, heading the interim government. He remained India's prime minister until his death in 1964.

Nehru took over at a time when India was reeling from the effects of the Partition of the Indian subcontinent into India and Pakistan. Thousands were dead and millions had been displaced. Besides, after being under foreign rule for centuries, India had become economically poor. To make things worse, just months after India got independence, Gandhiji was assassinated, and the morale of the country was very low. He had to make India a modern, independent nation. It was a daunting task.

Nehru launched agricultural and economic policies, as well as social policies that included basic primary education and meals for children. He introduced the Five-Year Plans to develop and industrialize the country. These plans might not have been perfect (as we now know, looking back) but they set India on the road to development.

Nehru had progressive ideas. He stressed the need for sustainable development (economic development without depleting natural resources) and was very particular that men and women should have equal rights. He reformed the Hindu civil code, and it enabled Hindu widows to enjoy equality with men.

India was split into India and Pakistan during

Independence but Nehru felt that just because there was already a separate Muslim state, it didn't mean that India would be a Hindu state. There were people from several different faiths and religions in India, and he wanted India to be secular. However, it has been said that his policies are not uniformly secular—that is, there aren't uniform laws for people of every religion.

Nehru played an important part in putting India on an equal footing with other countries on the global stage. He had modern ways of thinking, and laid great emphasis on learning and scientific discovery. He coined the term 'scientific temper', to describe an attitude or a way of life that involves using reason, logic and a scientific method of evidence-based thinking and acting. Nehru felt this was essential in the modern world, and that for India to succeed, Indians must develop a scientific temper. In 1976, scientific temper was included in the Indian Constitution as one of the fundamental duties of every Indian citizen.

Nehru put his ideas into action too. He was responsible for supporting the launch of a number of world-class educational institutions, like the All India Institute of Medical Sciences, the Indian Institutes of Technology and the Indian Institutes of Management. Some of the graduates from these institutions have gone on to make their mark on the world in their own ways.

These institutes helped fuel India's Information Technology revolution. Just when the field of IT was opening up, and the world was realizing how much potential there was in it, India had scores of qualified engineers who were ready at the right place and the right time, and helped make India an IT superpower.

Nehru also supported the founding of organizations like the Indian Space Research Organization—whose much-admired space programme is currently among the best in the world—the Defence Research and Development Organization the Atomic Energy Commission, the public sector units for heavy manufacturing, and many others. He had the good sense to provide them with the full support of his government. This led to India's industrialization and development in science and technology. It might not be an exaggeration to say that Nehru's foresight has put India where it is now on the global map.

Along with being the prime minister, Nehru was the foreign minister of India too. His foreign policy had a great impact on the world, and there was a time when he was a leader and spokesperson for several countries.

Nehru didn't trust foreign powers. And that's natural! India's fingers had been badly burnt

Panchsheel, or the Five Principles of Coexistence:

1. Mutual respect for each other's territorial integrity and sovereignty.
2. Mutual non-aggression.
3. Mutual non-interference in each other's internal affairs.
4. Equality and cooperation for mutual benefit.
5. Peaceful co-existence.

before. So, he tried to help construct a state that was self-sufficient, industrialized and socialist. He developed a policy of 'positive neutrality'—cooperating with everybody, and not taking sides. At that point, the Cold War was on between two major power blocs (combination of countries with a similar purpose), led by Russia and the US. They were hostile to each other, but not involved in actual warfare. Nehru was determined to protect India's independence by making sure it didn't come under the influence of either bloc. He co-founded the Non-Aligned Movement, a group of states that are not formally aligned with or against any of the major power blocs. These states were mostly former colonies that didn't want to depend on any major power. He became their key spokesperson, and developed Panchsheel—the five principles of peaceful coexistence, as part of the Non-Aligned Movement.

Nehru was an authoritative voice internationally. His position and attitudes on the international stage gave India the image of a distinctive, independent, international entity. This was important to India, after being subdued for centuries and not having its own voice. It helped create a positive image of India in the eyes of the world.

Nehru was a champion of world peace, and he worked tirelessly towards it. He was also a critic of racism and imperialism.

He worked hard for unity and solidarity between Africa and Asia. He believed that both African and Asian countries shared problems created by colonialism, and strived to enable and assist these exploited countries to become independent and self-reliant.

Nehru believed in internationalism (political and economic cooperation among nations) and felt that it is essential for understanding between governments. This was why he believed strongly in the necessity of the United Nations, and thought that it could have a greater role in promoting world peace, and has often been credited for the United Nations' continued existence.

Nehru was involved in several steps to solve problems that could come in the way of world peace. He spoke out strongly against racial discrimination and colonialism. He said that disarmament, especially nuclear disarmament, was one of the most pressing needs of the day, if peaceful coexistence had to be maintained in the world.

Nehru tried to mediate in several situations that he felt could explode into a third world war. He tried to maintain peace in Korea during the Korean war, by sending Indian troops. He was involved in peacekeeping efforts in Congo. He mediated between England and Egypt in the Suez Canal crisis, and played a role in getting Netherlands to leave Indonesia. Though, through his actions, he alienated the US, he became increasingly known as a world statesman and was frequently consulted on international matters by world leaders.

He envisioned a new world based on racial equality, world peace and economic development. He wanted to maintain friendly relationships with all the countries in the world, especially with India's neighbours.

Nehru, however, suffered several setbacks.

He faced conflict with Pakistan over Kashmir. Nehru sent troops to Kashmir to support the state's claim that they want to stay in India, but it didn't work. He had to call in the United Nations to negotiate a ceasefire, but there is a part of Kashmir that is still called Pakistan-occupied Kashmir. And to this day, Kashmir is deeply unstable.

The Sino–Indian war of 1962 was a major blow to him. Nehru had let down his guard with China, and misread China's intentions, even proclaiming 'Hindi-Chini Bhai-Bhai' (Indians and Chinese are brothers). When China launched an offensive against India, India retaliated, but Indian forces were beaten back. This was a shock to him, and had an impact on his already declining health, and he died in 1964.

mother teresa

26 August 1910–5 September 1997

Who: Roman Catholic nun, spiritual icon, humanitarian

How she changed the world: Founder of the Order of Missionaries of Charity, awakened a feeling of social responsibility in millions around the world.

WITH HER WRINKLED FACE, FOLDED PALMS AND THE familiar white sari edged with blue stripes, Mother Teresa is one of the most recognizable figures in the world.

Her name is synonymous with selfless service. Across the world, thousands have been inspired by her to help those in need. World leaders and movie stars have been influenced by her to get involved in charity and humanitarianism. And of course, contestants in beauty contests, in the hope of some extra points, righteously mention her name when asked about the person they most admire or want to emulate!

Mother Teresa was of Albanian descent, born in Skopje, in what is now the Republic of Macedonia. Her name at birth was Agnes Gonxha Bojaxhiu. Her father, a grocer, died when she was very young, and her mother inculcated in her a sense of charity. Even when she was a child, Agnes was influenced by stories of the lives of missionaries. When she was twelve, she heard the call of God, and decided that she would follow a religious life and become a missionary herself.

When Agnes turned eighteen, she joined an Irish community of nuns known as the Sisters of Loreto. She received training and instruction at the Institute of the Blessed Virgin Mary in Dublin, Ireland, for a few weeks. Then, she travelled to India and started working at one of the missions. Two years later, she took her initial vows as a nun. For the next seventeen years, she taught in St Mary's High School for Girls in Kolkata. This was a school for poor girls, run by the Order of Sisters of Loreto. She became the principal of the school. During this time, she took on the name Teresa. After taking her final vows of nunhood in 1937, she came to be known as Mother Teresa.

The Bengal famine of 1943 and the violence in India leading up to Independence left behind a lot of poor, sick people. Their plight moved Mother Teresa. She decided to dedicate her life working for the poor.

Mother Teresa took permission from the Church, left the convent, and started the Order of the Missionaries of Charity in 1948. The aim of the Order was to look after people whom nobody else was prepared to look after—the unloved, the unwanted and the shunned. She took Indian citizenship, and gave up the black habit of the Sisters of Loreto in favour of a sari. She got some basic medical training and then plunged into working with the poor and the sick. She had a band of other members around her—former teachers and students from St Mary's. She started an open-air school where she taught students by writing on the ground with a stick. For a while, they had to beg for funds, but as their work started being noticed by locals as well as politicians and organizations, funds started trickling in.

In 1952, Mother Teresa started Nirmal Hriday, a hospice where the poor and destitute could die with dignity. Over the next two decades, she opened numerous centres for the blind, the aged and the disabled. She started orphanages and nursing homes, and created a separate community for people with leprosy, so that they could live in peace, without suffering the scorn of society.

Over the years, Mother Teresa's fame spread, and attention was drawn to her work. She started missions all over the world. By the 1970s, the Order was helping orphans and those affected by poverty, disability, addiction, old age and disaster all over the world. There are now more than 700 missions operating in nearly 140 countries.

World leaders and celebrities flocked to meet her, and she received large contributions of money from all over the world. She inspired thousands of others to wake up to their social responsibility.

In 1979, she was awarded the Nobel Peace Prize for her work to overcome poverty and suffering, which are obstacles to peace.

She has also been bestowed with awards by countries all over the world, including the Congressional Medal of Honor and the Ramon Magsaysay award among others. India awarded her the Padma Shri in 1962 and the Bharat Ratna in 1980. Studies and polls show that she has been the most admired person in the world for decades. She was canonized in 2017 as Saint Teresa of Calcutta.

Mother Teresa has come under severe criticism both during her life and after her death. Many people believe that she shouldn't have been sainted. They feel that she wasn't worthy of it.

Mother Teresa has been accused of glorifying poverty and pain. In spite of the millions in charity that her Order received, visitors to her health centres have been appalled at the lack of hygiene, unavailability of food, and bad medical care. She refused to give pain medication to the ailing, because she felt pain was 'beautiful' and that it was a 'gift from god' and that it brought humans closer to god. But when her own health failed in later years, she chose the best medical treatment abroad, and so, she has been questioned for her hypocrisy.

Studies have shown that the liberation and education of women is the best way to end poverty. But Mother Teresa's beliefs about what women should or shouldn't do, were ancient and old-fashioned, and would ultimately not lead to the improvement of the lives of women. For instance, she has opposed abortion and divorce.

Mother Teresa has also been accused of mismanagement. Her Order refuses to provide audits of how they spend the millions that they receive in charity, and the condition of their centres seem pathetic in spite of receiving all that money.

Walking into a War Zone

In 1982, the Israeli army laid siege to the city of Beirut in Lebanon. Mother Teresa visited the convent of the Missionaries of Charity in East Beirut to help the local community. Here, she heard that children with physical and learning disabilities were stuck in a bomb shelter in West Beirut and were running out of food and water. This meant she would have to cross the Green Line, a dangerous war zone separating East and West Beirut to get to the children. Ignoring warnings, Mother Teresa daringly crossed over the heavily armed Green Line with a convoy of Red Cross vehicles and rescued the children, and brought them back to the Missionaries of Charity Convent in East Beirut.

She also received money and honours from known fraudsters and despots, and did not criticize them (or return the ill-gotten money) even after their crimes were proven.

Besides, there is another problem that makes many people uncomfortable. They say that her image in the world is built upon the standard picture of a 'white' person being the saviour of 'brown' people—it highlights the feeling of white supremacy that is present in society.

However, there is no denying the tremendous influence she has had. Mother Teresa died in September 1997, revered by people around the world. The Missionaries of Charity is continuing her work. The scale of her charitable activities and the millions of lives that she touched, both directly and indirectly, is phenomenal. Her zeal, dedication and commitment has inspired many to walk the same path.

These words by her are worth following—'Not all of us can do great things. But we can do small things with great love.'

subrahmanyan chandrasekhar

19 October 1910–21 August 1995

Who: Astrophysicist

How he changed the world: Nobel Laureate in Physics, the Chandrasekhar Limit is named after him.

THERE HAVE BEEN TIMES WHEN THE MOST DESERVING people have not been awarded the Nobel Prize—like Mahatma Gandhi, for example, the 'apostle of peace'. Some have been overlooked, some deliberately sidelined. But there is one case where a scientist's research was given its due recognition only fifty years after he first made the discovery. Thankfully, it wasn't too late. S. Chandrasekhar won the Nobel Prize in 1983, at the age of seventy-three, for a discovery that he had started thinking about when he was still in his teens!

It was the year 1929. Nineteen-year-old Chandrasekhar stood on a ship that was carrying him from India to Cambridge University in England. He had a pencil in his hand, and he made detailed calculations on a piece of paper. He felt his heart lift—he believed that he had figured out something significant, something that would shake the world of astrophysics, which was, at that time, still in its infancy.

Chandra, as he was popularly known, had always been a brilliant student. He was born in Lahore, where his father, an accountant general with the British government, was posted. They later moved back to Madras (now Chennai), in Tamil Nadu, where they were originally from. Chandra grew up in a house surrounded by books. He was caught up in the patriotism that accompanied the freedom struggle, and he felt that by doing well in science, he would prove to the world what Indians were capable of. Besides, he was inspired by his uncle, the famous scientist C.V. Raman, who had just discovered the Raman effect (and would get the Nobel Prize the following year).

Chandra was extremely enthusiastic about his future. He had studied popular books by Arthur Eddington, and had taught himself about stars and the basics of astrophysics. He had already published papers, finished his graduation, and now he was on his way to Cambridge on a Government of India scholarship.

At that time, scientists believed that when a star reached the end of its life—that is, after it converts all the hydrogen in it to helium—it loses energy, cools down and contracts under the influence of its own gravity to a size approximately that of the sun. These extremely dense stars are called 'white dwarfs'. Chandra wondered what would happen if he applied Einstein's Theory of Relativity to stars. This made sense to him—after all, the particles inside stars travelled at speeds that were close to the speed of light—and Einstein's theory had to be applied in this situation.

His calculations showed him that a star that is more than 1.44 times the mass of the sun, will not become a white dwarf. Instead, it will continue to collapse, blow off its gaseous envelope in a supernova explosion, and become a neutron star. Stars that are even more massive would go on collapsing internally, until they reached a tiny point of infinite density, with a gravity so high that nothing can escape them, not even light. These, as we know now, are black holes, but they were not called black holes back then. This was the first time anybody had predicted the existence of black holes.

Chandra went to Cambridge, and showed his work to R.H. Fowler, a British physicist and astronomer, whom Chandra had been in touch with, and who had helped publish his first paper. Chandra expected to be welcomed with praise and glory. But to his disappointment, nothing like that happened. Finally, he sent his findings to the US-based *Astrophysical Journal*, in which it was published. But the discovery was largely ignored.

Chandra was disappointed. But he settled down to study. It wasn't easy. He had no friends, nobody to talk to. The forbidding weather of England, in contrast to the warm, sunny weather of his home in India, made it worse for him.

But Chandra kept working, and finished his PhD in 1933. After that, he applied for a fellowship in Trinity College, and to his surprise and delight, he got it. He continued to work on theoretical astrophysics.

At this time, Sir Arthur Eddington, the same person whose books had influenced Chandra in his teens, came to know about Chandra. Eddington started visiting Chandra in his rooms, and taking an interest in his work.

Eddington was a world-famous figure, a respected astrophysicist, and a populariser of science. More than a decade before, Eddington had undertaken an adventurous expedition to West Africa to measure the deflection of starlight by the sun during a total solar eclipse. These measurements had proven Einstein's general theory of relativity. Thanks to this, Einstein immediately became a world icon, and Eddington became known throughout the world. He was the one to actually establish the field of astrophysics.

Chandra was naturally delighted and flattered that Eddington was taking such an interest in him. They had some excellent conversations, and Chandra truly enjoyed Eddington's company. Eddington encouraged Chandra to lay forth his results at a conference of the Royal Astronomical Society in London. Chandra delivered his paper, showing that above a certain mass, a star would dwindle to nothing. He sat down. Eddington was slated to speak next and Chandra assumed Eddington would speak in support of his theory. Imagine his shock when Eddington rose to speak, and with the help of his famous oratorical skills, completely rubbished twenty-four-year-old Chandra's entire theory! The audience laughed and pitied Chandra.

Eddington's arguments against Chandra made no sense, but Eddington's fame and reputation were such that nobody dared disagree with him. In fact, over the next few years, many scientists privately wrote to Chandra and expressed their agreement with and support for his theory. But nobody spoke out aloud on his behalf as they did not want to side with an unknown person like Chandra against an intellectual giant. On two more platforms, the same thing happened. Why exactly did this eminent scientist take such pleasure in demolishing this young man? One reason of course was that it was opposite to what Eddington's own theory was. But nobody really knows why he did what he did.

In spite of the crushing betrayal and humiliation Chandra felt, he kept his professional animosity aside, and maintained a respectful friendship with Eddington.

So, this meant that even now, nobody bothered with Chandra's discovery. Chandra felt that if he continued to fight for his discoveries in the face of these obstacles, he would just be wasting time. So, he decided to leave this behind. He moved to the University of Chicago, where he carried out research in other fields of astrophysics, such as energy transfer by radiation in the atmospheres of stars, and on convection on the solar surface. He received several awards and recognition: the Gold Medal of the Royal Astronomical Society, the Royal and Copley Medals of the Royal Society, the National Medal of Science, and many other honours.

Finally, decades later, in 1966, scientists proved that black holes do exist, and in 1972, Cygnus-X1, a binary star system, provided major evidence for the existence of black holes. And now, Chandra's work was recognized. Since he had discovered that stars bigger than 1.44 times the mass of the sun were the ones that wouldn't turn into white dwarves, this number has come to be known as the Chandrasekhar Limit.

In 1983, Chandrasekhar shared the Nobel Prize in Physics with Dr William Fowler (who was honoured for his study of how elements are formed.)

Chandra was also a great teacher, and there is a story of how he travelled 75 miles from his observatory to Chicago and 75 miles back to teach a

A New Discovery

On 10 April 2019, the world got to see the first photo of a black hole. The image shows a bright ring of fire around a circular black hole, similar to what was predicted by theoretical calculations. This black hole is three million times the size of the earth, and 500 million trillion km away from earth in a galaxy called M87.

The picture was captured with the Event Horizon Telescope, a network of eight linked telescopes across the world. Dr Katie Bouman, a twenty-nine-year-old computer scientist, developed the algorithm that made this image possible.

class that consisted of only two students. Apparently, it was worth it, however, because those two students went on to win Nobel prizes!

He was also particular that he should help the scientific community. He was the editor of *Astrophysical Journal* for nineteen years. This in itself was a very demanding job, and yet, he did it along with his other writing and research commitments. He wrote several books, including a condensed version of Newton's Principia for lay people.

Subrahmanyan Chandrasekhar died in 1995 of a heart attack. According to his wishes, his Nobel Prize money was given away to support upcoming astrophysicists in the University of Chicago.

pandit ravi shankar

7 April 1920–11 December 2012

Who: One of India's foremost musicians, sitar virtuoso, accomplished composer.

How he changed the world: He popularized Indian classical music in the West, and influenced musicians all over the world. Often called the Godfather of World Music.

The sitar: the instrument you hear in the background in old Bollywood movies when finally something good happens to the hero after a series of misfortunes. Usually accompanied by the actor shedding tears of joy.

The sitar: also the instrument you hear in the background in Western documentaries and movies, whenever India is mentioned, or there is a scene set in India.

Indian classical musicians use dozens of instruments, but the reason the sitar is universally associated with India, could be because of sitar maestro Pandit Ravi Shankar, who introduced and popularized Indian classical music around the world.

The interesting thing was that Pandit Ravi Shankar originally started off as a dancer. He was born Rabindra Shankar Chowdhury in Varanasi on 7 April 1920. His older brother Uday Shankar was a dancer and choreographer who ran a very popular dance troupe. Ravi Shankar joined the troupe when he was ten years old. He learned to dance, and play various instruments in accompaniment to the music for the troupe. He travelled with the other members of the troupe across India, Europe and the US, performing at various prestigious stages. By the time he was fifteen years old, he was a star dancer, accustomed to a lot of attention and a luxurious life.

He came in contact with a number of Western audiences, and observed their reactions to different kinds of music and rhythms. He was exposed to quite a bit of Western music and he absorbed the musical traditions of the West as well.

But most of the Westerners who came to meet him and his brother often mentioned that Indian music sounded good only when it was played as an accompaniment to dance. Otherwise, they said, it was just repetitive and monotonous. It made Ravi Shankar furious. But at the same time, he felt sorry for them. Indian music was so rich and they had no idea at all! He felt he had to do something to change their perception—he had to introduce Indian classical music to them, show them how beautiful it was. But how would he do that?

At about that time, Ustad Allauddin Khan, who was the court musician of the Maharaja of Maihar, joined the dance troupe for a short while, and played the sitar solo as accompaniment to dance. Ravi Shankar was impressed by him. But the opposite wasn't quite true. Allauddin Khan thought that Ravi Shankar did have talent but was wasting it, and didn't know music well enough.

'Then teach me,' said Ravi Shankar. 'I want to learn music from you.'

But Allauddin Khan was sceptical. 'Alright,' he said. 'But only if you completely quit dance and the worldly life that you're leading, and immerse yourself in music. Besides, you have to come live with me.'

Ravi Shankar agreed. He sold his Western clothes, returned to India, and moved into Allauddin Khan's home. It was pretty common back then for students to live in the homes of their gurus. From a life of luxury in the big cities of the West, he had to live in a remote village full of mosquitoes, bedbugs, lizards and snakes. Besides, training under Allauddin Khan was rigorous. He often taught his students for eighteen hours a day! But Ravi Shankar studied hard. Finally, Allauddin Khan was pleased with his student.

Ravi Shankar started performing in India. He composed music for ballets for theatre in Bombay. He became the director of All India Radio, New Delhi, and formed an orchestra for which he composed music in which he combined Western and Indian music as well as musical instruments.

Ravi Shankar then started performing abroad. He held a number of popular concerts all over Russia, Eastern Europe and the United States, and became more and more famous internationally. During this time, he started writing music with the great American violinist Yehudi Menuhin. They made many albums together, one of which won the Grammy award (he would go on to win several other Grammys!).

Ravi Shankar was known for his charisma. Besides, his childhood experiences, and knowledge of how Westerners approached music, helped him put across Indian music to audiences in a way that everybody would understand. That helped Indian music become popular among non-Indian audiences. He started the Kinnara Music school, first in Mumbai, and then in Los Angeles in US.

His fame skyrocketed after he became associated with the Beatles, who were really popular at the time. George Harrison, one of the Beatles, had discovered the sitar and studied it in detail under Ravi Shankar, and used the sounds of the sitar in several songs.

Both the sitar and Ravi Shankar became familiar to listeners, and the rock-music scene of the 1960s was full of sitar sounds.

But Ravi Shankar wasn't too comfortable with this sudden fame. It also made him sad that his music came to be associated with drugs and hippie culture. He was horrified when, at some concerts, the audiences turned up completely stoned. 'You don't need drugs to get high,' he said to them. 'Listen to the music, I'll give you the same high with my music.' But they didn't listen. There were times when he walked off the stage in the middle of the show in disgust and disappointment. Coming from a culture where music is respected and almost revered, he viewed this as a gross disrespect, and it bothered him tremendously.

But on the other hand, his fame helped him collaborate with the best musicians in the world to make more beautiful music.

Ravi Shankar worked with the Jazz saxophonist John Coltrane, who was impressed with the Indian raga system, and even named his son Ravi in honour of Ravi Shankar. Robbie Krieger of The Doors, the conductor Andre Previn of the London Symphony Orchestra, musician John-Pierre Rampal and composer Zubin Mehta were some others that he worked with. Ravi Shankar taught the composer Philip Glass the development of music in Indian classical music, and the rhythmic structure (taala). He collaborated with Glass on the album *Passages*. The mixing of such different types of music resulted in new sounds that had never been heard before, and listeners loved that.

During the 1971 Bangladesh war, large-scale violence left thousands of Bangladeshis dead, injured and homeless. As if that wasn't enough, there were floods in the country. To aid in relief work for them, Ravi Shankar and George Harrison organized the 'Concert for Bangladesh' in Madison Square Garden in New York, for charity. Along with Ravi Shankar and Harrison, Bob Dylan and Eric Clapton, who were the top superstars of that time, performed. The proceeds from the concerts went to UNICEF for relief work in Bangladesh, and as a bonus, the recording of the concert won a Grammy in 1973.

Ravi Shankar also composed music for acclaimed movies, like *Anuradha*, Satyajit Ray's Apu Trilogy, and Richard Attenborough's *Gandhi*, for which he got an Oscar nomination.

Ravi Shankar spent his whole life representing the artistic traditions of India to the world. He was open to other traditions. He was so confident and well-versed in his own musical tradition, that he had no hesitation in engaging with music from other cultures. He was an informal cultural ambassador of India.

In India, traditionalists often accused him of diluting the purity of Indian classical music. But he disagreed, claiming that classical music had been changing over the centuries, and it is just that the changes were faster now. Besides, he said, as a composer, he experimented widely, but as a performer, he stayed true to his roots, especially as he grew older.

Ravi Shankar died in 2012 in San Diego, California. His daughters Anoushka Shankar, a sitar player, and Norah Jones, a Grammy-winning singer and songwriter, carry on his musical legacy.

In India, he was bestowed with the Padma Bhushan, Padma Vibhushan, the Kalidas Samman

Pandit Ravi Shankar's Five Grammy Awards

- 1967: Best Chamber Music Performance—**West Meets East** (with Yehudi Menuhin)
- 1973: Album of the Year—**The Concert for Bangladesh** (with George Harrison)
- 2002: Best World Music Album—**Full Circle: Carnegie Hall 2000**
- 2013: Best World Music Album—**The Living Room Sessions Part 1**
- Lifetime Achievement Award at the 55th Annual Grammy Awards

and the Bharat Ratna. Among other international honours, he got the Ramon Magsaysay award and five Grammy awards.

But in spite of all his achievements, he believed he never could truly be a master of music or his instrument. In an interview, talking about the vastness of music, he once said: 'It is like driving through a mist. The more you drive, the more you realize the road is still out there.'

har gobind khorana

9 January 1926–9 November 2011

Who: Biochemist, Nobel Laureate

How he changed the world: Cracked the genetic code, created the first synthetic gene.

WHAT IF YOU WON THE NOBEL PRIZE, AND WERE one of the last people to find out about it? That's what happened to Har Gobind Khorana. He was at a rented cottage by a lake, working on research papers, and had no phone with him. His wife had to drive all the way to inform him.

But nobody who knew him was surprised by that. They all knew him as a modest, humble man, who kept to himself, avoided publicity and hated speaking on telephones. But he was also a brilliant scientist, who came from an extremely poor background, and who completed his entire education with the help of scholarships. His story—from life in a remote village to becoming a scientist who cracked one of the most important codes ever and won the Nobel for it—is a lesson in sheer hard work, determination and focus.

Har Gobind Khorana was born in Raipur, a village in present-day Pakistan, which was then a part of India. His father was a patwari, an agricultural taxation clerk in the British government in India. He was determined that his children should be educated, and Har Gobind's first lessons were under a tree in his village. They were so poor that when his father bought him a pencil, he would break it into half and ask Har Gobind to use one half at a time in order to make it last longer.

Har Gobind studied in a high school in Punjab. He got a scholarship to study in Punjab University, Lahore, but he had to attend a mandatory interview before he could get admission into the university. But he was too shy to attend the interview, and didn't turn up at all. The admissions committee, however, was so impressed with his application that they went ahead and gave him admission anyway. So Khorana got a bachelor's, and later a master's degree in science from Punjab University.

Then, he got a Government of India Fellowship to study at the University of Liverpool, UK. The scholarship was for agriculture, to study insecticides and fungicides, because the government thought it might be useful, and that he could come back to India and put all the information to use. But it was 1945, World War II had just ended, and agriculture had become top priority everywhere. So, the university was full of people who had taken up all the spots in agricultural research. So, Khorana ended up studying chemistry instead, and got a PhD. His supervisor for his PhD was Roger J.S. Beer, who also looked after Khorana, and gradually introduced him to Western culture.

When he was studying, Khorana realized that it wasn't enough to just be good at science. If he wanted to be understood by other researchers, and if he wanted to make his work known to everybody, he would need to communicate it well. But his English wasn't that good. So, Khorana stayed up nights, listening to BBC broadcasters on the radio, and trained himself to speak slowly and with the right emphasis.

He later did his post-doctoral studies at a university in Zurich, Switzerland, with Professor Vladimir Prelog, who influenced him deeply. He did not earn any stipend, though, and had to depend on his savings for his day-to-day needs. To avoid spending on accommodation, he even secretly started living in the lab. Finally, Cambridge University funded his expenses, and then gave him a fellowship to go and work with them.

At around this time, James D. Watson and Francis H. Crick were working to find the structure of the DNA at Cambridge University. It was an exciting time in research, and Khorana became interested in the proteins and nucleic acids that make up DNA.

Dr Gordon M. Shrum of British Columbia Research Council in Vancouver, Canada, invited Khorana to join them in 1952. 'We don't have too much money or facilities,' said Dr Shrum, 'But you'll have all the freedom in the world to do whatever you want.' Khorana accepted, moved to Vancouver, and worked on a number of research projects in proteins and nucleic acids in the cell, and his work came to the attention of scientists around the world.

In 1960, he moved to the Institute for Enzyme Research in the University of Wisconsin, where his lab had researchers from the fields of chemistry, biology, enzymology and biochemistry. He himself was a biochemist, applying his knowledge of chemistry to the field of biology. Such a multi-disciplinary lab was rare in those days.

It was here that he conducted his work that led to his winning the Nobel Prize in Physiology or

The Nobel Prize for Work on the Structure of the DNA

Rosalind Franklin was a scientist working at King's College, London. She and her assistant Raymond Gosling took X-ray diffraction images of the DNA. Franklin's colleague Maurice Wilkins gave Watson and Crick these images without Franklin's knowledge. It was with the help of one of these pictures that Watson and Crick were able to conclusively determine the double helix structure of the DNA. For this discovery, Watson, Crick and Wilkins were awarded the Nobel Prize for Physiology or Medicine in 1962. By this time, Rosalind Franklin had died (at age thirty-seven) and as Nobel prizes are not given posthumously, she wasn't included in the prize. But even if she had lived, it is uncertain whether she would have been included in the Prize, as her contribution to the discovery had been swept under the carpet.

Medicine in 1968, along with Robert W. Holley of Cornell University and Marshall W. Nirenberg of the National Institutes of Health. All three worked independently, to show how genetic information is translated into proteins, which carry out the functions of a living cell.

Wait, what?

Let's start from the beginning. DNA (deoxyribonucleic acid) is a complex molecule that contains the instructions that the organism needs in order for it to live, grow and reproduce. Every cell in the organism has DNA (organized into chromosomes), and it is passed on from parents to children.

The DNA is further made up of molecules. These are called nucleotides. A nucleotide = a phosphate group + sugar group + nitrogen base.

If you think of the DNA structure as a kind of spiral ladder, the phosphate group and sugar group form the sides of the ladder, and the nitrogen base forms the rungs.

The four types of nitrogen bases are Adenine (A), Guanine (G), Cytosine (C) and Thymine (T).

The order or sequence in which these bases are present is what determines the instructions of the DNA, or the genetic code. You can think of them as letters in an alphabet making up words. These genes tell the cell how to make proteins.

But how do they 'tell' the cells what to do? That's where the RNA (ribonucleic acid) comes in. So, what the other researchers found was that a stretch of DNA that contains instructions for making a protein is copied to make a similar stretch of single-stranded RNA. This is like a mirror image of a DNA. This strand of RNA floats over to a ribosome (another kind of molecule), where another RNA strand reads the first one. This second RNA strand in the ribosome then assembles amino acids in the proper order—and thus it constructs a protein; amino acids are thus the building blocks of proteins. It is almost like the second RNA reads an instruction manual of protein building, and the ribosome is like a factory floor!

What was Khorana's role in this? The first thing Khorana did was to confirm that the way the four nucleotides A, G, C and T are arranged indeed determines the function of a cell.

Then, with the help of chemical synthesis, he showed that the nucleotide instructions are transmitted to the cells in groups of three called codons, and each such codon represents a specific amino acid. He and his group then figured out which serial combinations of nucleotides form which specific amino acids. They made up an entire list of these combinations.

Finally, he also found that some of these codons was a code to tell the cell where to start and stop reading code. Like punctuation marks!

This was a big deal! It opened the doors to a lot of research, and all the genetic research that is being done all over the world now, is based on Khorana's research.

He didn't stop there. In 1972, Khorana had another breakthrough. He constructed the first artificial gene. Four years later, he was able to get an artificial gene to function inside a bacterial cell.

This breakthrough, the ability to synthesize DNA, resulted in major advances in genetic engineering and the development of the biotechnology industry.

In 1970, he moved to MIT in Cambridge, where he

worked on biological membranes and bioenergetics and other such areas, until his death in 1971.

Har Gobind Khorana was also an excellent teacher and mentor. He mentored more than 150 postdoctoral researchers and several graduates. Many of his students went on to be eminent academics, and worked in biotech industries and government services. For example, one was involved in the decoding of the human genome (the complete set of genes present in a cell). Another won the 1993 Nobel Prize in Chemistry. Khorana published more than 450 scientific research papers.

Among other honours, he was awarded the National Medal of Science (for which the White House had to track him down with difficulty to confirm that he would attend the award ceremony, because he wouldn't answer his phone).

One of his favourite quotes was: 'We must be modest, except in our aims.' Har Gobind Khorana's life is a great example of this philosophy.

faqir chand kohli

b. 28 February 1924

Who: Indian businessman and engineer

How he changed the world: Father of the Indian software industry—made invaluable contributions to the inception and growth of the Indian IT and software-export industry.

IF YOU WANTED A COMPUTER, WHAT WOULD YOU do? Tell your parents, do some basic research on the type and model of laptop you want; then maybe your parents would worry a bit about the expense, but you'd go ahead and buy it. Right?

Can you believe there was a time when it was next to impossible to buy a computer in India?

But now, India is, and has been a forerunner in the software industry for the last few decades. In India, it is a ₹15,000-crore industry. More than 60 per cent of what India exports to the US is software.

So how did it all begin? How did India turn out to be a global giant in the software industry?

It started with someone you've probably not even heard of.

Faqir Chand Kohli was born in Peshawar (in present-day Pakistan) and studied in Punjab University in Lahore. In 1946, he went to Ontario, Canada and studied electrical engineering in Queen's University. After working there for a while, he studied in Massachusetts Institute of Technology in Boston, US, and got a master's in electrical engineering.

In 1951, he returned to the country. India had recently become independent, and Kohli wanted to help in building a modern, successful and independent nation. He joined Tata Electric Companies, a part of the Tata group of companies.

At this time, he got to know Dr P.K. Kelkar, an academic, with whom he collaborated in improving engineering education. When Kelkar became the founding director of IIT Kanpur, he asked Kohli to help him recruit faculty members for the institute. Kohli himself gave some lectures there, in addition to working at his regular job at Tata Electric Companies.

During this time, IIT Kanpur received an IBM 1620 computer as a gift from a consortium of American universities. A bunch of computing professionals came to India and gave the students and the professors an introductory course in computing. This was Kohli's first introduction to computers. He participated enthusiastically, and recognized the value of computers.

There was a large computer in Tata Institute of Fundamental Research. Kohli worked on it for a while. Fired up with excitement about the potential of computers, he hit upon the idea of introducing computers to control the power grid that served the city of Mumbai. It was a pioneering idea—but buying a computer was very, very difficult back then.

Computers were seen as luxuries, and it was assumed that computers would steal human jobs, depriving people of their livelihoods. So the government had put a number of restrictions on importing a computer. And even if you somehow did manage to get permission to buy one, you would have had to pay through your nose.

Kohli needed to get around the problem. He knew that if he said he wanted a computer for purposes of research, then it would be easier to buy one. So that is what he did. With the help of this 'research' computer, Kohli successfully computerized Mumbai's power grid. It was the first power grid in Asia to be computerized. Even in the US, only a handful of utilities had been computerized before this.

The bigwigs at Tata realized that Kohli was onto

something big. So, in 1964, they appointed him the general manager of Tata Consultancy Services (TCS), an information technology company.

Kohli set out to acquire some more computers. He was able to buy one for cheap from a firm that wanted to get rid of their computer. The company's labour union had objected to the computer because it would take away jobs. So the company was glad to get rid of it. He leased two IBM computers, and then he set about computerizing the operations of some of the fifty-plus companies under the Tata name.

Now he tried to get business from customers outside the Tata group. This was not at all an easy task. Firstly, the advantages of computerization were little-known. And even if some private companies were interested, they couldn't buy computers, for the same reason that Kohli couldn't. However, he managed to computerize the operations of Central Bank of India, and Mumbai's telephone directory.

In 1973, Kohli was elected to the board of directors of the Institute of Electrical and Electronics Engineers (IEEE). He was the first Indian to be chosen for this honour.

Now, he had global contacts, and he set about getting overseas assignments.

He went to Detroit, US, and met the people from Burroughs, a computer manufacturer. Burroughs wanted TCS to develop an operating system for a new computer series. But TCS didn't have a Burroughs

The IT Boom in India

By the late seventies, several other Indian companies started operations in the IT field. Western India Vegetable Products limited (which was established in 1945), renamed itself Wipro Limited when it started IT and computing operations in the late seventies and early eighties. Infosys was established soon after, in 1981.

Later, in the nineties, many more companies, including HCL Technologies and Cognizant sprung up to take advantage of the potential of the information technology field.

computer. It would mean a delay of at least two years if they waited to import a Burroughs computer. So, his team at TCS wrote the software using the computer that they had (an ICL computer), and then wrote another filter software that would make the ICL software work on the Burroughs computer. They sent this to Burroughs, and it worked!

This was the first ever win for India's software industry (which was almost non-existent then). Burroughs was highly impressed. Not only did they now have the operating system they needed, they could also convince users of ICL computers to migrate to Burroughs! Double win!

TCS now got a constant stream of work from Burroughs and its associates, and the Burroughs team got TCS some more software development contracts, for instance, from the Detroit Police Department.

TCS then opened its first overseas office in New York. Inspired by the success of TCS, other software companies in India jumped onto the bandwagon, and after that, there was no looking back for the Indian software industry.

Kohli led research and development in his organization. But he realized that it wasn't enough if he just guided his own company towards a better computing future. For business to grow, much more was needed—the necessary infrastructure, and the right kind of atmosphere in the country. This also involved persuading the government to open its eyes to the potential of this industry in creating jobs, and thus make it lift its restrictions on computers and look ahead into the future. So that is what he worked towards.

With more and more companies entering the software industry, a momentum was created that made the government realize that it needed to create a favourable environment and invest in research and infrastructure. Restrictions were removed in the early nineties, and then, the software industry boomed.

Now companies abroad could outsource their software-related work to India. This turned out to be less expensive for these foreign companies than getting the same work done by people in their own country. These companies, in turn, could offer their products for lesser price than their competitors. So, their profits increased, and they grew. Thus, more and more companies started outsourcing their work, and more countries started offering software services. The international scene changed tremendously. The business world would never be the same again!

Kohli headed a number of computer and business-based organizations in India such as the Computer Society of India, IEEE, Nasscom and others.

Kohli, now in his nineties, is still active. He is working to use computers and communications to aid adult literacy. He has created software that uses images and sounds to teach complete words to illiterate adults, before teaching them the alphabet. This has proved to be really successful as adults became literate in a matter of months, enough to read newspapers. This method has been implemented extensively in Andhra Pradesh, and is spreading across different states, making lakhs of Indians functionally literate.

He also feels that a majority of Indians who do not know English, and carry out their business in Indian languages, are losing out on benefits of computerization. So, he is encouraging programming and software development in Indic or desi languages so as to have computers in Indian languages. This way, more people in India can fully make use of and benefit from computers.

He was honoured with the Padma Bhushan in 2002.

narinder singh kapany

b. 31 October 1926

Who: Physicist, Entrepreneur, Educator, Philanthropist

How he changed the world: Coined the term 'fibre optics', and popularized this technology.

Ever wondered about the Internet? About how large amounts of information are transferred from one point to another? If you've been on a curving, tube-like water slide at an amusement park, bouncing off the walls, and then landing in the water with a splash, you are already on your way to understanding how it works.

The Internet uses optical fibres to transfer information coded into a beam of light from one point to another.

A fibre optic cable is a bundle of optical fibres—incredibly thin strands of glass or plastic. A human hair is as thick as ten of these strands put together. Each cable has multiple strands and can carry a huge amount of information—for instance, millions of telephone calls at one time.

Light travels down an optical fibre by reflecting off the walls in a way that is somewhat similar to water flowing down a curving water slide at an amusement park. You can think of yourself as the information and the water as the beam of light. So, in the same way that the water transfers you from the top of the slide to the bottom, the light carries information from one point to another.

And it's not just the Internet that is made possible because of optical fibres. High-speed communication, high-capacity broadcasting, endoscopy, laser technology—all these wouldn't have been possible without the field of fibre optics.

But who invented optical fibres and created an entire industry based on fibre optics? There is no one person—research and studies by a bunch of scientists over the years perfected this technology. But the person responsible for coining the term 'Fibre Optics', and spreading the word about it is Narinder Singh Kapany.

Kapany was born in 1927 in Moga, Punjab. When he was in high school in Dehradun, his father gave him a Kodak box-camera. This kick-started his interest in optics, as he was curious to learn about how it worked. At around the same time, a teacher told him that light travels in straight lines. 'That can't be right,' thought Kapany, and kept thinking about it as he went for higher studies.

Kapany studied in Agra University, and then

Box Camera

A box camera is a basic, simple box-shaped camera, with a lens at one end, and film at the other.

It works the same way as a human eye. When a shutter in front of the lens is opened, light (which is reflected from the object being photographed) passes through the lens. This lens inverts the image, and projects the inverted image onto light-sensitive film on the other end of the camera. This film can be developed into a photograph.

These cameras work best in bright sunlight, when the subject is stationary, and at the right distance from the box camera (as you cannot focus using this camera.)

worked as an officer in the Indian Ordnance Factories Service, the industrial wing of the defence forces of India. There, he designed and manufactured optical instruments. He tried bending light using right-angled prisms.

Kapany wanted to learn more about optic technology. So he travelled to London to study the subject at the Imperial College of Science and Technology. In 1952, he got a graduate assistantship with the English physicist Harold Hopkins, with a grant from the Royal Society. Here, he started studying bending of light.

Light bending wasn't a new idea. Back in the 1840s, scientists Daniel Collodon and Jacques Babinet had demonstrated that light could be directed along the arcs of a water fountain. Some years later, John Tyndall shone a light into a tank of water. The pipe carrying water out of the tank, carried light with it in an arc.

But now, Hopkins suggested that Kapany could try using glass cylinders to bend light. Kapany started studying how to make glass fibres and aligned them together so that they would transmit both images and light. At this time, the main intention was to use optical fibres as an endoscope—a medical instrument using which doctors could see inside the human body without having to cut it open. After some research and experimentation, Kapany and Hopkins managed to send a simple picture down a light pipe made up of thousands of glass fibres.

Kapany and Hopkins published a paper in *Nature* in 1954, 'A Flexible Fibrescope, Using Static Scanning', where they described their results.

In the same issue, scientist Bram van Heel published an article on cladding. If this cladding was used to line the fibres, it would prevent reflected light escaping from the glass fibres and make the image clearer.

Kapany now realized that these optical fibres have a lot of potential.

In 1955, Kapany presented his findings to his professor. He felt he had finished what he had come to do, and was preparing to go back to India. From an early age, he had wanted to be an entrepreneur, and so he wanted to start his own factory in India. He had even met the then prime minister Jawaharlal Nehru, who had asked him to be the Scientific Advisor to the Ministry of Defence, and he was thinking about it.

But his professor convinced the University of London to approve Kapany for entry into the PhD programme, and convinced Kapany to stay on in London and start writing his PhD thesis. But Kapany liked hands-on and practical work. He wanted to 'do' things, and so, he wasn't too keen on a PhD. He thought that doing a PhD would make him an 'egghead'! Later, he realized that he had been wrong.

In 1955, Kapany completed his PhD in fibre optics, the first in that field. The next year, he went to a conference in Italy to present a paper about fibre optics. There, he met an American professor who convinced him to move to the University of Rochester in the US as a faculty member.

So, Kapany went to the US and joined the university. Along with being a teacher, he also became a consultant for the eye-health products company Bausch and Lomb. He built optical devices, did some research and obtained patents. Most importantly, he spoke and wrote extensively about fibre optics. In 1957, he moved to the Illinois Institute of Technology Research Institute. By this time, he was the best-known spokesperson in the world for fibre optics.

He published an article 'Fiber Optics' in *Scientific American* in 1960, in which he wrote, 'If light is directed into one end of a glass fibre, it will emerge at the other end. Bundles of such fibres can be used to conduct images over a tortuous path and to transform them in various ways.'

Kapany wrote dozens of scientific papers and published the first book on fibre optics—*Fiber Optics: Principles and Applications* in 1967. His name became associated with the term Fibre Optics. So, although a number of other scientists studied, researched extensively and contributed to the field, it is Kapany who was responsible for popularizing it and making the term familiar to everybody. He is frequently referred to as the Father of Fibre Optics.

In 1961, Kapany started the company Optics Technology in California. His company built one of the first lasers used in laser surgery. The company also mass-produced helium-neon gas lasers. He later started Kaptron Inc, and K2 Optronics, to conduct research and innovation in the fields of communications, lasers, biomedical instrumentation, solar energy and pollution monitoring.

Kapany taught extensively too, at Stanford, University of California Berkeley, and University of California Santa Cruz. At UC Santa Cruz, he has endowed a chair in optical electronics.

In 2009, Charles Kao was awarded the Nobel Prize in Physics for his work in fibre optics. Kao had proven years ago that telephone signals could be transmitted across hundreds of kilometres using very pure optical glass fibres. This laid the foundation for high-speed Internet that now allows for the exchange of text and images across the world in a fraction of a second.

Some people were surprised that Kapany was ignored for the Nobel Prize, but Kapany himself shrugs it off, saying that it is the decision of the Nobel committee, and that they must have had a certain criterion to choose the names they did.

Kapany is a distinguished fellow of numerous scientific societies, including the British Royal Academy of Engineering, the Optical Society of

America and the American Association for the Advancement of Science, and a member of the National Inventors Council.

Fortune magazine recognized him as one of seven 'Unsung Heroes' in their 'Businessman of the Century' issue in 1999.

Kapany is a philanthropist too. He founded and is the chairman of the Sikh Foundation that runs programmes in publishing, academia and art. He has donated a large sum of money to the Asian Art Museum in San Francisco to finance the Sikh art collection.

amartya sen

b. 3 November 1933

Who: Economist

How he changed the world: Nobel Laureate in Economic Sciences. His work on human rights, poverty and equality changed the way governments deal with famines.

AMARTYA, A NINE-YEAR-OLD BOY, WAS AT SCHOOL, playing with his friends. It was two years before World War II ended, and India was four years away from getting independence. The Great Bengal famine of 1943 had just hit his homeland. But Amartya was clueless about all that. He was from a well-off family, and he was happy in his little world.

Suddenly, a man wandered by the school. He seemed deranged and confused. Amartya asked the man if he needed help. To Amartya's shock, the man told him that he hadn't eaten for forty days. This man wasn't the only one, though. In the next few days, thousands of starving people stumbled by on the way to Kolkata looking for charities who could feed them.

Amartya's grandfather gave him a small cigarette tin, and told him to measure out rice from it and give it to each family that passed their home. Amartya did so, but was disturbed and affected by all that he saw.

Three million people died in the famine. Those who suffered most were landless rural labourers,

The Bengal Famine of 1943

Nearly 3 million Indians died in the Bengal famine of 1943, of starvation and diseases caused by malnutrition and lack of healthcare. Millions more were impoverished and displaced.

Research has shown that this was an entirely 'man-made' disaster. Conditions in the Bengal region were already bad in 1941, before the 1943 drought. But Britain refused to acknowledge that the situation was serious. As part of the war effort, Winston Churchill, the then prime minister of Britain, ordered that food from starving Indians be diverted to British soldiers and stockpiles in Britain and Europe, though they were already well-supplied. Churchill also confiscated huge supplies of rice from the coastal regions of Bengal so that Japanese armies, in case they invaded India, wouldn't have access to resources. This set off a series of shortages that led to the famine.

the poorest of the poor. Amartya went on to study poverty and famine and how it can be prevented, and fifty-five years later, he won the Nobel Prize for his work.

Amartya Kumar Sen was born in 1933 in Shantiniketan, in the Vishwabharati campus founded by Rabindranath Tagore. Tagore gave him the name Amartya. His grandfather taught Sanskrit and ancient Indian culture there, and Sen's father was a professor of chemistry in Dhaka university. Sen began his schooling in Dhaka, Bangladesh, studied for a while in Burma, and then moved back to Shantiniketan.

Shantiniketan was a progressive school, and it gave importance to developing curiosity about the world, rather than academic excellence and competitiveness. It merged Indian culture and Western beliefs, and was open to all kinds of influences.

In his teens, he wondered if he should study Sanskrit or mathematics or physics, but later settled on economics. But he never once doubted what he wanted to be—he was sure he would be a teacher and a researcher.

Sen then studied in Presidency College, Calcutta, after which he went to Trinity College in Cambridge where he got another BA.

He was diagnosed with cancer of the mouth when he was in Presidency College, and was treated with a high dose of radiation (at that time, it was still not known what doses were safe) and it killed the bones of his palate. In Cambridge, he underwent surgery to reconstruct the bones.

He came back to India, and was asked to set up the department of Economics in Kolkata's Jadavpur University when he was only twenty-three! It created a storm. Graffiti appeared on the walls suggesting that the new professor had just been snatched from the cradle. Undaunted, Sen worked there for two years, and then went back to Cambridge, this time to get a PhD.

After that, he plunged into the world of academia, and lived and taught at various universities around the world. According to him, he has spent most of his life in campuses (having even been born on one—Shantiniketan!) and has taught in Kolkata, Cambridge, Delhi University, the London School of

Economics, Oxford University, Harvard University, and was a visiting professor at MIT, Stanford, Berkeley and Cornell.

Sen's field of research and study has mainly been on welfare economics. What kind of effects do the economic policies of a government or a ruler have on the well-being of the community? Do they help improve the lives of the citizens, especially the poorest members of society? Or do they create more difficulties for the poor?

In 1970, Sen wrote a monograph (a detailed, written study) titled 'Collective Choice and Social Welfare'. It has gone into history as an important and influential work. It inspired researchers everywhere to address the issues of basic welfare. Sen devised new methods of measuring poverty, and with the help of this information, the economic conditions of the poor could be dealt with in a better, more informed way.

He studied inequality in detail. He explained why there are more men in poor countries than women. Sen figured out that boys receive better health treatment and better opportunities in life than girls, and so more boys grow up into adulthood. He wrote a widely read article that says that there are 100 million 'missing' women in the world, killed (so to speak) just by discrimination!

He also studied the causes of the Bengal famine of 1943 in which millions died.

If you were asked what a famine is, what would you say? 'Shortage of food' would be the most obvious answer, correct? Caused due to natural consequences, like droughts, and floods, maybe?

Sen doesn't agree. He compared the food supply in 1941 when there was no famine, and in 1943 when there was a famine—and he found there was not too much of a difference in food production. In fact, there was enough food supply in India at that time, and nobody should have gone hungry. So what happened? The problem was that there was not enough or efficient distribution of the food. And why was this? Because the poor, especially rural labourers, had lost their jobs and so couldn't afford to buy the food that was available.

He also studied the famines of Sahel, Ethiopia and China, and concluded that in many cases of famine, it is not food supplies that was reduced. Even if food supply did reduce because of drought or other natural causes, there was enough food in the rest of the country. Or the country had enough money to import food from outside. So the real factors were social and economic factors—reduced wages, unemployment, rising food prices—and this is what led to starvation among some members of society.

This study caused a revolution in organizations around the world. Suddenly, governments and international organizations who were working on food crises, realized that they had been approaching it the wrong way. They had been focusing only on providing immediate aid, for example, by directly distributing food to those who were affected. Now the policy makers realized that they should also look into ways in which they can replace the income that the poor have lost—and to make sure that food prices remain stable.

Sen said that if a country wants to improve economically, it should first introduce social reforms—for example, improvement in public health and education. Then economic growth will follow.

Sen worked on measuring poverty. Previously, poverty index just measured the number of people below the poverty line. But Sen's measurement takes into account how poor the average poor person is, and how resources are distributed among the poor. With these measurements, the poor can be assisted in better ways.

Sen isn't politically outspoken, and has several times refused the offer of governments to be their advisor. Yet, he has had a major influence on politics. He has advised and shaped the work of international bodies such as the United Nations' International Labour Organization. He helped create the United Nations' Human Development Index to compare welfare between countries. This has become the most accurate and reliable international index, used universally.

Amartya Sen was awarded the Nobel Prize in Economic Sciences in 1998 'for his contribution to welfare economics'. With part of his Nobel money, he founded the Pratichi Trust, which is committed to education, healthcare, nutrition and gender equality in India.

Sen has written more than twenty books and 200 articles. He is the first Asian to head an Oxbridge college, as a Master of Trinity College, Cambridge. He is also a very inspiring professor and lecturer. Not only has he lectured in the most prestigious universities, he has more than fifty honorary degrees.

Sen is also a pioneer of studies in gender equality. When referring to an abstract person, he always makes sure to use 'she' or 'her' instead of 'he' or 'him'.

Sen has been a permanent resident of the US for fifty years, but he has chosen to retain his Indian citizenship. He is currently working as a Professor of Economics and Philosophy at Harvard University.

Sen has been given several awards and honours, including the National Humanities Medal and the Bharat Ratna.

venkatraman ramakrishnan

b. 1952

Who: Scientist

How he changed the world: Nobel Laureate in Chemistry who discovered the structure of the ribosome.

IF YOU EVER THOUGHT THAT ALL SCIENTISTS discovered their interests early in life, and worked in the same field with unwavering focus before they made their splendid discoveries—here's a slightly different kind of scientist story for you!

Venkatraman Ramakrishnan, known popularly as Venki, was born in Chidambaram in Tamil Nadu. Both his parents were scientists, and ever since he was a young boy, the family had scientist visitors dropping in from India and abroad. So, Venki grew up with science all around him. He also realized early on that science wasn't just something that you do all by yourself, but that it is an international enterprise, that it involves collaboration with scientists from around the globe.

Venki got the National Science Talent Search Examination scholarship from the Government of India to study science and he got his bachelor's degree from Baroda University in Gujarat. Then he flew to the US, studied at Ohio University and got a PhD in Physics in 1976, researching ferroelectricity.

But even as he worked towards his PhD,

something nagged at him. Nothing new and exciting seemed to be happening in the world of physics, whereas he kept hearing of one advancement after another in the field of biology. He decided that he wanted in on the action too.

He had to start at the beginning—to understand the basics of biology, and so he enrolled for another PhD, this time in the University of California San Diego. Here he studied cell membranes. After two years, Peter Moore, an expert at ribosomes in Yale University, offered Venki a post-graduate position in his lab. So off Venki went, and started studying the ribosome.

A ribosome is a small particle inside the cell, consisting of RNA and other proteins. Proteins are created inside ribosomes. A ribosome consists of two units—one small and one big. Venki learnt to use a technique called neutron scattering to study the small unit of the ribosome of the bacterium Escherichia-coli (if this name sounds familiar, it is because one kind of E-coli causes stomach upsets).

Here, he learned some specialized scientific techniques used to work with ribosomes, and later, these techniques helped him in his Nobel prize-winning research. Later, he continued studying the structure of the ribosome, with another technique called X-ray crystallography in Brookhaven National Laboratory in New York.

In 1991, he took a sabbatical of one year, and on a Guggenheim Fellowship, flew across the Atlantic to England, to work in the Laboratory of Molecular Biology (LMB) in Cambridge. He learned how to use a synchrotron to find out the structure of protein crystals.

Here at LMB, he learnt two important lessons. The people at LMB were not content to work on ordinary, routine problems in science. They were challenging themselves, pushing the horizons and asking difficult questions and thinking up creative ways to solve them. They knew that they might not find the answers anytime soon, but that didn't stop them. Secondly, he saw that even very famous scientists didn't hesitate to ask trivial questions. He learnt that ignorance is nothing to be ashamed of, and if you need answers, no question is too stupid to ask.

Venki went back to Brookhaven, excited to work more. But unfortunately, the funds he received for his research kept decreasing. So he moved once again, this time to the University of Utah, where he started working again on the sub-unit of ribosomes. But the more he worked, the more he realized that LMB had everything he wanted—technical experts, continuous funding, and the freedom to do what he wanted to.

So, once again he hopped on a plane back to Cambridge University, England, where he joined the LMB, even though he would be paid less than what he was being paid in the universities in the US. But he knew what was important to him. He wanted to be in a place that had a reputation of tackling very hard problems. It might take ages to solve the problem, and he was okay with that. Besides, most importantly, he could be sure that they wouldn't suddenly cut off his funding and resources if things weren't going well.

He got to work again, and after a lot of research, he published a series of papers in which he put forth the data on the RNA structure, and drew up a detailed structure of the small unit of the ribosome in the bacteria Thermus thermophilus (this bacterium is commonly used in genetic research).

At one point, after a particularly spectacular day of work and some good results, Venki started dancing around in the lab, saying, 'We're going to be famous!'

And he was right.

It was for this work that he was awarded the 2009 Nobel Prize in Chemistry with Ada E. Yonath and Thomas A. Steitz, 'for having showed what the ribosome looks like and how it functions at the atomic level.'

Wait—chemistry? That's right. Though the ribosome and the cell are in the realm of biology, the study of the structure and the function of the ribosome involves chemistry.

When Venki got the call from the Nobel committee telling him that he had won the prize, he thought he was being pranked by one of his friends, and complimented the caller, saying that he was doing a pretty good imitation of a Swedish accent! The joke was on him, however, when he realized that the Swedish accent of the caller was quite real, and that he'd actually won the prize!

However, Venki is not very happy with the way the Nobel Prize works. He says that it lessens or ignores the contributions of those dozens of researchers who toiled alongside the final winners. These collaborators would also have contributed in many ways but they are not given any recognition, which he feels is unfair. He also thinks that the Nobel Prize in the sciences made sense a hundred years ago when science and the way people worked were completely different from what it is now. At that time, scientists largely worked in isolation. Today's science is very collaborative, he says, and so, to turn it into a contest and give out prizes is wrong.

Venki's prize-winning research has immediate, important applications. His structure of the ribosome revealed to us how antibiotics attack bacteria (antibiotics are chemicals used to kill bacteria or prevent them from reproducing). Many antibiotics target the ribosome of the bacteria, but also end up affecting human cells. The structure of the ribosome of a bacterium is different from the ribosome of a human. You can imagine antibiotics like lego blocks. By developing antibiotics that can fit only into the ribosome of the bacteria, but not into the ribosome of a human cell, we can avoid damaging human cells. That way, antibiotics can be more efficient.

Another result of this work is that it solves one of the chicken-and-egg problems of the scientific world. If ribosomes are needed to make proteins,

The Nobel Controversies

Ever since its inception, the Nobel Prize has been controversial. Every year, critics note that the prize has overlooked some of the most important contributors in certain fields. The Nobel prizes have been accused of being biased against women too—Lise Meitner, for instance, contributed to the discovery of nuclear fission, but only Otto Hahn, her colleague, got the Nobel.

and if ribosomes themselves are made of protein, then which came first? The answer is that the active core of the ribosome is the RNA. The proteins might have come in later. So, the ribosome is 'an RNA-based machine that evolved the ability to make proteins'.

Venki is now working on another kind of ribosome: the eukaryotic ribosome. A eukaryotic cell is a cell that has a nucleus, for example, human cells. A prokaryotic cell does not have a nucleus. Example, bacteria. This eukaryotic ribosome is a complex machine and to conduct research on it, it would need a lot of drive and determination. But that's something Venki already has. He is a hiker, and he says that during hiking, sometimes you have to keep going even if you are exhausted. In the same way, the hiker's endurance is useful during long scientific projects, when you have to keep going even when the end is not in sight.

In Venki's new book *Gene Machine: The Race to Decipher the Secrets of the Ribosome*, he tells the story of his journey to discover the inner workings of the ribosome.

Venki was elected a member of the US National Academy of Sciences in 2004 and a foreign member of the Indian National Science Academy in 2008. In 2015, he was elected the president of the Royal Society for a five-year term, and is the first Indian-born person to hold that position. Venki received the Louis-Jeantet Prize for Medicine in 2007, and the Heatley Medal, awarded by the British Biochemical Society, in 2008. He has also been knighted.

indra k. nooyi

b. 28 October 1955

Who: One of the top executives in the world, the highest-ranked woman of Indian origin in corporate America.

How she changed the world: Inspired millions of women to break the corporate glass-ceiling.

When Indra and her sister were children, their mother played a dinner-time game with them. She would ask both of them to write a speech about what they would do if they were prime minister, or president—a different world leader each time. After the allotted time, they would each have to deliver the speech, and their mother would decide for whom she would vote that day.

This little game was fun when they played, but without knowing, it gave Indra the confidence that she could be anything she wanted to be.

Growing up, Indra Nooyi was always quite the rebel and the rule-breaker. She was from a conservative family, and belonged to a society that was full of traditional ideas. People around her had strong opinions about what was right and what was wrong for women to do. But Nooyi didn't care about these rules. After all, as long as she wasn't causing anybody harm, what was wrong in doing what she thought was fun? In college, she played cricket in an all-girls' team. She was the lead guitarist and singer in a rock band while doing her bachelor's degree in

Madras Christian College. Both these were activities in which girls in her circles hardly ever participated.

Nooyi was a good student, and after her undergraduate studies in science and mathematics, she got an MBA from Indian Institute of Management, Calcutta.

Nooyi worked for a while in India, and one of her first jobs was as a brand manager at Johnson & Johnson, where she worked in the Stayfree account. It was a challenging position because at the time, India still didn't allow advertising for personal hygiene products—so how would she get the word out to those who might want to buy these products? She solved the problem by reaching out directly to female students in colleges, and getting them to try the products themselves.

But after working for a while, Nooyi started feeling that there was still a lot left for her to learn. So she applied to universities in the US for higher studies. She was accepted into the master's degree in Public and Private Management at Yale University's Graduate School of Management. She flew to the US in 1978, once again something that made the conservative people in her circles clap their palms to their mouths—young women in her conservative, middle-class circles didn't do such things! Going alone to the US? Now who would marry her?

Cola Wars

Coke has traditionally portrayed itself as a family drink, invoking nostalgia. Pepsi has tried to brand itself as a youthful alternative, which tries to keep up with the social changes in every generation. Both companies have scrambled to sign up the biggest celebrities of the day, sponsor the most popular sports teams in each country, and create clever ads that take digs at each other. The cola wars really heated up in 1975 when Pepsi ran ads in which consumers showed a preference for Pepsi over Coke in blind taste tests.

Studying at Yale was good, but the financial aid she received wasn't enough for her daily expenses. So, Nooyi had to work nights as a receptionist at a hotel in order to make ends meet. But she worked hard, and she graduated from Yale.

Nooyi worked at Boston Consulting Group, Motorola and ABB. Her work with ABB was impressive, and it brought her to the attention of several corporate leaders like Jack Welch of GE, and Wayne Calloway of PepsiCo. They all wanted her to join their companies.

Nooyi chose PepsiCo, the soft drink giant. And in 1994, she joined as senior vice president of corporate strategy and development.

The Coke vs Pepsi rivalry has been one of the biggest battles in the industry for decades, each trying to better the other, to come up with cleverer advertising and better products. The rivalry is even known as the cola wars.

At the time Nooyi joined Pepsi, Coke had the upper hand, and so the task before Nooyi was quite big. She had to make sure that Pepsi got into the competition again. She made huge changes in the structure of the company, and introduced several new brands under PepsiCo. She also started working on strategies that would help the company expand and grow better in the future.

At the time, Pepsi owned KFC, Pizza Hut and Taco Bell. She put these three under a newly created company called Tricon Global Restaurants. This turned out to be a good decision for Pepsi. It is now called Yum! Brands, and is one of the world's largest fast food restaurant companies.

Nooyi is said to have a sharp mind and a good insight into how the market works. The market keeps changing, and the company needs be on its toes constantly. It is not easy, because the market is very complex. People want to be healthy. But at the same time, they want to have fun. They know that junk food is not good for them, and yet they want to eat and drink a lot of junk food. And of course, the companies want to make customers buy their products. So what should they do? How should they handle all these new trends?

When Nooyi observed that customers were becoming aware that they should eat healthier foods, she decided that her company should produce more healthy drinks and foods. PepsiCo acquired Tropicana, the fruit juice company, and then bought Quaker Oats for more than 13 billion dollars. This is a massive figure. People in the industry raised their eyebrows. Was this a good idea? Turned out that it was. Through Quaker Oats, PepsiCo also got control of the highly popular energy drink Gatorade. So, these decisions turned out to be extremely profitable for PepsiCo.

In 2001, Nooyi was named CFO of the company. Five years later, she became the CEO. And then, the year after that, she became the chairman of the board as well.

Nooyi has acknowledged that her industry is linked to one of the biggest public health challenges of the world: obesity. It affects millions of people, and even very young children have started suffering from severe obesity. This affects both their mental and physical health. That is also one of the reasons that Nooyi has tried to bring in more healthy products. She classified her company's products into three kinds: 'Fun for you' (potato chips and soda), 'Better for you' (diet sodas, low-fat versions of snacks) and 'Good for you' (oatmeal). She has invested more money in the healthier products. She has even tried to improve the healthiness of the 'fun' stuff—by reducing the portion sizes, for example.

When she saw that modern snackers are looking for organic and healthy snacks, Nooyi started investing in hummus and guacamole snacks, cold-press juices, and other such healthier options. Customers are also trying to avoid sugary drinks, and so drinking less and less soda. So PepsiCo tried to increase diet sodas and healthier drinks.

Nooyi gained global acclaim for her strategy and insight. She has won several awards and recognition. *Forbes*, *Fortune*, *Time* and other magazines have included her in lists of the Most Powerful Women in Business, Most Influential Women in the World, and Best Global Business leaders, and so on. India awarded her the Padma Bhushan in 2007.

Nooyi stepped down as CEO of PepsiCo in August 2018, and continued as chairman until February 2019. In February 2019, Amazon named her the new member to Amazon's board of directors, and appointed her to the audit committee of the board.

Nooyi says that she will continue working towards creating an atmosphere where people from diverse backgrounds are welcome in the corporate world. Just like she, a woman, and of Indian origin, broke barriers to become one of the top executives in the world, she wants to make sure that others get that chance too. She also strives to create more roles for female leaders, and ensures that more and more women are encouraged to rise to top positions.

Nooyi broke another barrier when she was appointed the International Cricket Council's first independent female director.

Nooyi's motto is 'Performance with Purpose'. Those who have worked with her say that she is highly innovative, hardworking and energetic. She is also a perfectionist, and encourages people to do their work as well as they can.

Nooyi advises young executives to take up the most difficult tasks early in their career. She says that you should work hard and in a focused way, so that when you join a company, people should see that you have arrived. Learn from everybody around you, she says, and listen and absorb more than you speak—that's the way to do the best that you can, and rise in your career.

kalpana chawla

17 March 1962–1 February 2003

Who: Astronaut

How she changed the world: The first Indian-origin woman to go into space; small-town girl who dreamed big, and inspired millions.

IN A SCHOOL IN KARNAL IN HARYANA, A MATHEMATICS class was in progress. The math teacher was teaching her students the concept of sets. A set is a collection of objects. She went on to teach them about a 'null set'.

'A null set is an empty set, a set that does not contain anything,' said the teacher. 'For example, a set of female Indian astronauts.'

One of the students raised her hand. 'Perhaps one day, that won't be a null set!' she said.

Everybody laughed. But little did they imagine that this same girl would one day grow up to be an astronaut herself, and that set would not be a null set any longer!

Kalpana Chawla was a bright, curious girl who loved looking at the sky. There was a flying club in their town, and the planes fascinated her. Often, she sat with her brother, gazing at the planes whizzing overhead. She liked watching the planes landing and taking off in the nearby field. She would ride her bicycle hard to see if she could overtake the planes speeding on the ground during landing and take-off.

Her father took her to the flying club, and to her joy, she got to ride on a plane and a glider.

As she grew, she became more and more fascinated with the sky and with space.

Chawla was very good in math and science. Generally, girls in her family and her town didn't study much. They got married early. But Chawla wanted to study, and she enrolled in aeronautical engineering at Punjab Engineering College. She was the first woman in this field. Her teachers tried to dissuade her, and tried to push her to go into some other line, but she was adamant.

It wasn't easy for Chawla at the college, though. There was no girls' hostel at all, and she lived alone in a tiny room, cycling to college every day.

But Chawla did well at college. Besides, she read a lot, learnt karate, and was the student editor of the college magazine. She also participated in the college aeronautics clubs.

After she finished her engineering, she wanted to go abroad to study further. She had a difficult time convincing her parents that it would be a good thing for her, but finally they relented.

Chawla studied aerospace engineering at the University of Texas in Arlington. After that, she got a PhD in aeronautical engineering in the University of Colorado in Boulder. She started working as a researcher for NASA (National Aeronautics and Space Administration).

Meanwhile, Chawla hadn't forgotten her childhood fascination for aeroplanes. She learned how to fly aeroplanes—and many kinds, at that. She had a commercial pilot's license for single and multi-engine land aeroplanes and seaplanes. She was also a certified flight instructor. She particularly enjoyed aerobatics (spectacular flying manoeuvres in the air.)

During her time in NASA, Chawla applied for the US astronaut programme. There were 4000 applicants for the same programme. In 1994, she became one of the twenty chosen to take part in it. Now she could get a chance to go into space!

After a rigorous training regimen, in 1997, Chawla was selected to fly on the space shuttle Columbia on flight STS-87 as a mission specialist and the robotic arm operator. She became the first woman of Indian-origin to go into space.

On board the STS-87, the crew members conducted several scientific experiments. They focused on experiments designed to study how things work in the weightless environment of space. The team had equipment to help observe the outer atmospheric layers of the sun. They collected a lot of important data.

The shuttle orbited the earth 252 times. That's a distance of 6.5 million miles in just two weeks!

There was a mishap, though. The crew released a sun-watching Spartan satellite, 3000 pounds in weight, from the space shuttle. But, it malfunctioned. So they decided to get it back into the shuttle. They would need to use the 50-foot-long robotic arm of the shuttle to catch it, and bring it back. Chawla was in charge of operating the arm. She tried to capture the satellite, but the arm did not latch on to the satellite. When she pulled back the arm, the satellite went spiralling out of control. They wouldn't be able to conduct any experiments now. But they needed the satellite back. After all, it cost 10 million dollars, and they could fix it and reuse it next time. They couldn't just let it float away in space. So, two astronauts from the crew had to go on a spacewalk to retrieve the runaway satellite.

Chawla thought that it was her fault that she couldn't catch hold of the satellite correctly, and that this was the end of her career. But after they came back to Earth, NASA investigated the incident for five months, and cleared her of any blame, when they found that other factors were responsible for the mishap.

In 2000, Chawla was chosen for her second voyage into space, this time on STS-107. The mission was delayed, and finally launched in 2003. It was a dedicated science and research mission. The crew worked twenty-four hours a day, in alternating shifts. Over sixteen days, the crew completed more than eighty experiments.

On 1 February 2003, the space shuttle started its journey back to Earth, to land at Kennedy Space Centre. But during the launch of the shuttle, a piece of insulation had broken off and damaged the thermal protection system of the shuttle's wing. This is the shield that protects the shuttle from excessive heat that is generated when the shuttle re-enters

India's Space Programme

Indian Space Research Organisation (ISRO), was formed in 1969. Since its inception, it has successfully launched several satellites that now orbit the earth. They are a part of our telecommunications infrastructure, survey our country's natural resources, monitor the weather and conduct scientific research.

ISRO's latest crowning achievement is the Mangalyaan or the Mars Orbiter Mission. This mission was spearheaded by a group of extremely talented and dedicated women scientists. Mangalyaan was launched into space in 2013 using a rocket built from indigenous technology. It was built within two years, and cost less than Hollywood movies about space. With it, India became the first nation to put a spacecraft into orbit around another planet in the first attempt. Mangalyaan has been sending us spectacular colour pictures of the red planet.

the Earth's atmosphere. So when the shuttle, on its way back, entered the Earth's atmosphere, the heat generated (because of the friction due to gases in the atmosphere) was too much for the spacecraft to bear. The wing broke up, and the shuttle became unstable. Within forty seconds, the shuttle depressurized (the gas inside the shuttle that keeps the shuttle at the right pressure, leaked out). The shuttle broke up. All the astronauts, including Chawla, died.

Chawla was posthumously awarded the Congressional Space Medal of Honor, the NASA Space Flight Medal, and the NASA Distinguished Service Medal. A street in New York has been named after her, and several institutions, buildings and scholarships in India and the world now bear her name. India also named its first weather satellite Kalpana-1 in her honour.

Kalpana Chawla dreamed big, and in her determination to achieve her dreams, she broke all the conventional barriers of society. She refused to be dissuaded from the path she wanted to take. She is the inspiration for millions of women and girls all around the world, who believe that if she could work towards her dreams and achieve them, then so can they.

Chawla had this advice for anybody with a big dream: 'The path from dreams to success does exist. May you have the vision to find it, the courage to get onto it.'

India's Contribution to the World

India has been an influencer long before the term was made popular by social media. Here are some ways in which ideas and innovations that came out of India have enriched and shaped the world over the millennia.

Ayurveda

Ayurveda is a traditional system of medicine that originated and developed in India about 3000 years ago. It focuses both on prevention as well as the cure of diseases. Ayu means life, and Veda is study. According to mythology, Dhanvantri, the divine physician, received the knowledge of Ayurveda from Brahma. Ayurveda has evolved over the centuries, and is practiced all over the world.

Ayurveda took shape long before microscopes were invented, and bacteria and viruses discovered. So, the Ayurvedic system of medicine does not recognize the existence of germs, and is not based on the treatment of diseases based on germ theory. The basic concept of Ayurveda is that the human body is made up of a number of different components, and an imbalance in these components create ill-health. So, Ayurvedic practitioners believe that by setting the balance right, the individual can be cured. It is considered alternative medicine.

Some of the home remedies that you take for a cold and a cough (turmeric and milk, ginger decoction, and so on) are loosely based on Ayurveda, and are not harmful when consumed in moderation. But some Ayurvedic medicines have been known to contain toxic heavy metals that can be fatal, so watch out!

The Bhagavad Gita

The *Bhagavad Gita* is the holy book of the Hindus, and a part of the epic Mahabharata. The book essentially advises the reader to be a good person, do their duty and not worry about the consequences or the fruits of their action. The wisdom in this book has appealed to writers, thinkers, philosophers and leaders all over the world, and has influenced their actions and decisions. In India, of course, thousands of people have been guided by the book, including leaders like Mahatma Gandhi. But the *Gita* is popular even outside India. It has been translated into more than a hundred languages, and millions of copies have been sold. Well-known people like Albert Einstein, Henry David Thoreau, T.S. Eliot, Annie Besant, Ralph Waldo Emerson, Aldous Huxley and others have all been influenced by the words of the Gita.

Buttons

The earliest known buttons were found in Mohenjodaro in the Indus Valley. They were originally used more as ornaments than for fastening. These buttons are made of curved shell, and are believed to be 5000 years old. They usually had flat decorative faces, which fit into a loop. They weren't found in straight rows, but individual buttons were placed here and there, perhaps to achieve a fashionable effect!

Chess

Chess originated in India about 1500 years ago. Some historians say that similar versions of the game have been played in China and other places, but current evidence shows that the earliest known version of chess in its current form, was first played in India. It was known as Chaturanga, which means 'Four arms'. Chaturanga is a term used in warfare. It denotes an army consisting of four parts—elephants, chariots, horsemen and foot soldiers. Chaturanga was a game of battle strategy, and consisted of an 8x8 board, with many pieces, each with different powers.

From India, the game spread to Persia, and then the Arabs borrowed it from them and took it to Europe. Chess is now played internationally, and is among the most popular games worldwide. India's own Viswanathan Anand is one of the greatest chess players in the history of the world.

Cotton

Cotton has been used in tropical regions for millennia. But the first written evidence of cotton is found in the Rig Veda, composed 3500 years ago, which indicates that cotton was already being cultivated in the Indus Valley region at that time.

A thousand years later, Greek historian Herodotus wrote about the cotton in India: 'There are trees which grow wild there, the fruit of which is a wool exceeding in beauty and goodness that of sheep. The Indians make their clothes of this tree wool.'

Cotton cultivation gradually spread across the world, but Indian cotton remained highly valued and sought-after for centuries afterward. Indian handloom cotton is still very popular all around the world.

Cricket

Okay, so cricket *might* have originated in England, but is there any other country that has embraced it like India has?

It is unlikely that international cricket would be

as popular as it still is, if not for India. As it is, only a handful of countries play it in the world. So how has the sport sustained itself at the international level for so many decades? It is estimated that India provides cricket with 80 per cent of the revenues that the sport needs. So yes, the reason that cricketing organizations and cricketers around the world are so wealthy is because of the money that India, with its massive audiences, brings in through advertisements, endorsements and other avenues. Also, the Board of Control for Cricket in India has a lot of control over what goes on in the game.

And of course, India's cricketers themselves have contributed significantly to the game, with players like Sunil Gavaskar, Sachin Tendulkar, Rahul Dravid, Kapil Dev, Anil Kumble, M.S. Dhoni, Virat Kohli and many others going down in history as all-time greats.

Crystal Sugar

Sugarcane evolved from grasses and began growing wild 60,000 years or so ago. It is believed to have first been domesticated in Polynesia, and from there, the knowledge spread to Southeast Asia. But sugarcane had to be eaten where it was grown, because if it wasn't fresh, it would dry up.

In around the 4th or 5th century CE, during the Gupta period, Indians discovered how to crystallize sugar. Now, it became easy to transport. So, sugar quickly became an expensive commodity that India exported along the silk route. The knowledge of sugarcane-growing then spread to the middle-eastern countries and to Europe, and later to the rest of the world.

The Epics and Indian Mythology

The Ramayana, written by Valmiki, and the Mahabharata, written by Veda Vyasa, are two of the most remarkable, magnificent, complex stories in the world. Brimming with colourful characters and fantastic events, they have provided endless entertainment and life lessons to generations of people all over the world.

Indians of course are only too familiar with them. But in any country where Hinduism had an influence, there are temples dedicated to gods and characters from the Ramayana and the Mahabharata. Each of these cultures has its own versions of these stories, with slight changes here and there—but all these cultures have made the epics their own, and have embraced it. The epics have influenced art, architecture and literature throughout India and Asia.

Films

India's film industry is the largest in the world, a multi-million-dollar industry producing more than a thousand films each year. Bollywood is the most well-known, but regional film industries are no less in their reach. Movies are big in India, but they've crossed the borders and influenced people in several countries. Raj Kapoor and his films were hits in the seventies in Russia and Eastern Europe. Rajnikanth is a huge icon in Japan. Superstars like Amitabh Bachchan and Shahrukh Khan are idolized in Afghanistan, Europe and beyond. Indian tourists to countries like Brazil, Egypt and many others, bring back stories of people stopping them on the streets and singing Bollywood songs to them!

Indian films have influenced the culture of other countries—their bazaars sell Indian clothes and Indian film music play in homes and restaurants. World fashion is changing thanks to Bollywood. Besides, Indian film stars are making it big in Hollywood. And A.R. Rahman's music is also hugely popular in Hollywood.

Bollywood music, and other genres of popular music are the rage everywhere. Bollywood dance is being recognized as a genre in itself and is being used in choreography internationally. Gyms even have Bollywood fitness routines that use songs from Bollywood and other popular Indian albums.

Indian movies have made their mark among film critics too. Directors like Satyajit Ray and Mira Nair have made acclaimed movies that have influenced other directors and film-makers.

Fine Arts

India is famed for its exquisite art and architecture, and its beautiful, complex, ancient classical music and dance. Shades of Indian art and architecture can be seen in other countries, especially in Southeast

Asia. Modern Indian artists and sculptors, like M.F. Hussain and others, have had their works exhibited in galleries and museums across the world, and their works have sold for millions of dollars.

Indian musicians and dancers have large followings across the globe. Dancers like Birju Maharaj and Rukmini Devi Arundale are known internationally. Ali Akbar Khan, Zakir Hussain, M.S. Subbulakshmi and other musicians have taken Indian music to the rest of the world. Several artistes are working with Indian music to achieve fusion music to the best effects.

Food

Arguably, India has the greatest variety of food in the world. India's food bursts with flavours, textures and tastes, and is a treat to the senses. Indian food has been studied by food scientists to see what makes it so delicious. The answer: Indian food has fewer overlapping flavours, unlike other cuisines that depend on complementary flavours.

Indian food has made its way out of India, acquired fans beyond its borders, and has influenced cuisines the world over. Indian cookbooks sell millions of copies. Some countries have adapted Indian tastes and dishes and in some cases, have made it their own. In fact, Chicken Tikka Masala, a British creation, is one of Britain's favourite foods. Chaat, samosas, curries, naan, dosas, idlis and vadas are also becoming increasingly popular around the world. Besides, Indian cuisine is being blended with other cuisines to achieve delicious results. Naanwiches, Burrotis and Indian Curry Pizza, anybody?

Indigo

Indigo is one of the oldest materials used to dye textiles. It was originally extracted from the plant Indigofera tinctorial, which is a tropical plant. Ancient India was the first centre for the production and processing of indigo. India supplied indigo to Europe through Arab merchants as early as 2000 years ago. It was a luxury item, and very rare. The Greeks called the dye indikon (from India), and the Romans started calling it indicum. Gradually, it came to be known as indigo in English.

India had a flourishing indigo industry until as

recently as the 19th century, with centres in Bengal and Bihar. Due to the high demand for indigo dye in Britain, the British forced Indian farmers to cultivate indigo for no profit, and the farmers protested in what is known as the Indigo revolt. The British planters were held guilty, and indigo cultivation came to an end. Now synthetic dyes (inexpensive and easy to use) have largely taken over.

Jute

Jute originated in India, and has been cultivated in India for centuries, especially in the Bengal region. Its primary use is for packaging agricultural and industrial materials. It is preferred because it is strong and cheap, safe, environmentally friendly and completely biodegradable.

The British exported raw jute to their country, and used it mainly to manufacture cordage (ropes, used in shipping). They set up a yarn manufacturing facility in Dundee, Scotland, and then in 1855, they set up the first jute mill in Rishra, West Bengal. After that, several more factories and processing centres were set up.

Now, jute is grown and processed in seven states in east India, with West Bengal growing the majority of it. India is the world's largest producer of raw jute and jute goods. Japan, Germany, UK, Belgium and France are the main importers of raw jute fibres.

The Indian Government has made it mandatory to use jute packaging for food grains and sugar. Jute is also used to make floor mats and area rugs. Fabrics, accessories and other personal-use materials are now also being made from jute, and its popularity is on the rise.

Language

India has contributed several words to the English language. Most of them were absorbed into English when the British in India picked up words from the local languages, and adapted them. Some of these words have fallen by the wayside, or are not used widely. But many of them have stayed on, and have made English richer.

Avatar, bandanna, bazaar, chutney, shampoo, guru, khaki, pyjamas, hullabaloo, loot, bandicoot, bangle, bungalow, juggernaut, jungle, mantra, pundit, veranda, cheetah, dacoit, karma, mantra, mogul, punch—are just some of them.

Literature

Apart from the great epics—Ramayana and Mahabharatha—India is a fountain of mythological stories and fables. *Panchatantra* and *Jataka Tales*, apart from the thousands of folk tales from every part of India, have gone out into the world for ages. They have inspired, and blended with stories from elsewhere, and taken new lives of their own.

In the modern age, there have been excellent writers of prose and poetry, and some of them have made their mark on the international literary scene. Rabindranath Tagore was a global literary star and won the Nobel Prize for Literature. Raja Rao, Mulk Raj Anand and R.K. Narayan were among the pioneers of Indian writing in English, and they gained international recognition for their work.

There are other lesser known writers too, like Dhan Gopal Mukherjee, the only Indian to have won the Newbery Medal in 1928 for his children's novel *Gay-Neck*.

More recently, Salman Rushdie, Vikram Seth, Arundhati Roy, Shashi Tharoor, Vikram Chandra, Aravind Adiga, Amitav Ghosh, Kiran Desai, Rohinton Mistry and many other writers have written globally acclaimed works that have won prestigious awards, including the Man Booker Prize. These writers have large fan followings across the world and their books have sold by the millions.

There are scores of brilliant writers who write in Indian regional languages. With their works being translated into English, they are gaining international recognition, for example K.R. Meera, Vivek Shanbhag and others.

Metallurgy

Metallurgy has a rich history in India. In the first millennium BCE, India's metallurgical skills were highly valued.

Copper was used in the 2nd and 3rd century BCE, and was used to make coins. Since metallurgy is invaluable for weapons, this science enjoyed the patronage of the kings, and that's why metallurgy continued to flourish in India even well into the modern era. The knowledge of this technology moved to the West through travellers and invaders.

The iron pillar at the Qutub Complex in Delhi is an example of the technical excellence reached in the 4th century CE by the Gupta dynasty. (The reason it doesn't rust is because of high quantities of phosphorous in it.)

India also contributed to zinc technology—our ancients prepared and used zinc much before the rest of the world. There is evidence of zinc ore mining in Rajasthan dating back to the 5th century BCE.

Number System and Zero

The Hindu Arabic numerals—1, 2, 3, 4, 5, 6, 7, 8, 9, 0—are the numbers of the decimal system. They evolved in India through the work of Indian mathematicians sometime in the 6th or 7th century BCE. Although the Mesopotamians and Mayans knew the concept of zero, it was not used as a number or in calculations. Zero was developed in India to use in conjunction with other numbers—and this was an earth-shaking event. It helped mathematicians move away from the old, cumbersome methods of counting. If you know Roman numerals, and if you have broken your head trying to write huge numbers with it, imagine doing mathematical calculations with it!

Zero and the decimal system might seem simple and commonplace to us now, but at that time, it changed the whole world of mathematics. Calculations became much simpler to do. This led to further advancements in mathematics, and as a result, in other fields of science.

A couple of centuries later, the Arab region became the centre of mathematics, as it was situated on trade routes between the East and the West. So, Arabic scholars received knowledge from both places, and supplemented it with their own knowledge. The Arabic mathematicians Al-Khwarizmi and Al-Kindi wrote about and used the decimal system. The Europeans read their work, and adapted the decimal system sometime in the 12th century BCE.

Since the Europeans learned it from the Arabs, they called these numbers Arabic numerals. But after modern scholars determined that they originated from India, the numbers are now referred to as Hindu–Arabic numerals.

The decimal system has since prevailed for general and scientific use throughout the world, because of its ease of use and its simplicity.

Polo

Polo is, to put it simply, hockey played on horseback. The origins of polo are uncertain, since it has been played for ages all over central Asia, including India. It was played by nomads, partly as a sport, and partly, as training for war.

But the modern version of the game originated in Manipur in India. It was called Sagol-Kangjei. British military officers and tea planters saw the local people playing the game, and were fascinated. They learnt the game from them, and called it polo, an anglicized term of the word 'pulu', which was what the locals called the ball. The British established the first polo club in Silchar, Assam in 1859. By 1876, the sport had spread all over the world, to Malta, England, Ireland, Argentina, Australia and North America. It is now played in nearly eighty countries.

Religion

India is the birthplace of four major religions—Hinduism, Buddhism, Jainism and Sikhism.

Hinduism evolved as a mixture of beliefs, cultures and traditions from all over the subcontinent. Scholars believe that it began about 4000 years back. There was no single founder, unlike other religions. The term Hindu started being used only a thousand years ago, and that too, by Arabic speakers, to refer to the inhabitants of the land across the Sindhu (the river Indus). Even until very recently, the term Hindu was used geographically, rather than in a religious sense.

The founder of Buddhism was the Buddha, and Sikhism originated through the teachings of Guru Nanak in the Punjab region. Jainism evolved in India through the ages, and like Hinduism, doesn't have a founder, strictly speaking. But Mahavira, a contemporary of the Buddha, reformed and popularized this ancient faith.

Spices

Talk about Indian food and the first thing you think

of is—spices! The liberal and creative use of spices in Indian food is one of the main things that sets it apart from other cuisines. The aromas that waft out of an Indian kitchen are heady, and can get you salivating no matter how full your tummy is. And of course, we are the experts of spice for a reason. Black pepper, cinnamon, turmeric and cardamom have been cultivated and used in India for thousands of years. Spices have been used not only in cooking, but in medicine as well, and make appearances in ancient medical treatises of Sushruta, Charaka and others.

Spices were perhaps the first products to be exported widely from India. It was in extremely high demand in the Arab and the Western world. And so, kingdoms vied with each other to establish trade routes to India. At one point, India was the country with the largest export and trading business in the world!

Both land and sea routes to and from India were hot links that resulted in the transfer of much more than spices—knowledge, culture and art. These trade routes changed the course of history in several ways—politically, culturally and in terms of knowledge. In fact, it was when Christopher Columbus set out to find an alternate spice route to India that he 'discovered' America.

In a way, spices could be said to have caused India's downfall too, for it was to trade in spices, among other things, that the Europeans came to India—and overstayed their welcome.

Textiles

Indian textiles have a long history of being popular all around the world. Indian textile makers have been exporting fabrics for centuries—to the Middle East, Africa, Asia and the Mediterranean.

Fragments of Indian cotton textiles have been found in archaeological sites in Jordan dated 6000 years ago! It was identified by its fibres and spinning method as originating in India. Pieces of cloth used for furnishing, tailored garments, and even the sail-cloth for boats and ships, have been excavated from sites in central Asia and the Middle East.

Indian weavers were skilled in spinning, weaving and dyeing. But more than that, they also knew their market. They knew that the bright flowery patterns that the West liked did not suit the Southeast Asian markets. To Southeast Asia (with which they had been trading for 2000 years), they exported block-printed cloth, woven silks, fabrics with delicate designs. For daily wear, they exported simple printed cottons. Similarly, they knew that Africa liked checked prints on their cloth. So they were smart enough to adapt their products according to the needs of the customers.

India already had a roaring trade by the time the first Europeans reached our shores. Over the next couple of centuries, India exported top quality cloth—muslin, calico, chintz, gingham—to Europe. The Indian textile industry continued to be one of the best in the world until the Industrial Revolution, when Britain started manufacturing inexpensive clothes and suppressed the Indian market.

Universities and Centres of Learning

Nalanda, Takshashila and Pushpagiri—centres of learning in the ancient world—were based in India.

Nalanda University was founded in the 5th

century CE. It had over 10,000 students who had come from Japan, China, Korea, Tibet, Persia and Greece. Nalanda was a hub of learning, with scholars absorbed in seminars and lectures, and engaged in heated debates.

Nalanda was a centre of Buddhist studies. This attracted the Chinese traveller Xuanzang, who studied there in the 7th century. In his works, Xuanzang talks about its library, which had nine storeys and 'soared into the clouds'.

But Nalanda didn't focus only on Buddhism. It also trained students in astronomy, fine arts, medicine, the art of war, secular studies, logic and mathematics, languages and public health. Nalanda was destroyed by invaders (and thousands of invaluable books burnt) in the 12th century. In 2017, it was re-established as a modern university in Rajgir, Bihar.

Takshashila (Taxila) was another popular centre of learning. It is not strictly considered a university, since teaching was conducted individually. It was established as early as 5th century BCE! Chanakya is believed to have written the *Arthashastra* in

Takshashila. It was destroyed by the Huns around the time that Nalanda was established.

Wootz Steel

The technology to make Wootz Steel, which was used to make swords of exceptional sharpness and toughness, originated in India. The name Wootz is a corruption of the word 'ukku'—the Kannada word for steel. This technology was passed on to Europe and the Middle East, where it became famous as Damascus steel.

In fact, during the British wars in India, under Tipu Sultan, the Indian soldiers had such good swords that British soldiers were instructed to stop and pick up the swords of fallen Indian soldiers because they were of such high quality compared to their own!

Yoga

Yoga originated in India around 2500 years ago. The Rig Veda has references to yoga too. Patanjali, a sage who lived in the 4th century BCE, studied and organized the knowledge of yoga from different yoga traditions, and compiled them into 196 Yoga Sutras.

Yoga has been practiced in India for a long time, but only in the 20th century did it become popular across the world. It started with Swami Vivekananda who introduced it to the West in the 1890s. But it really caught on only after the 1970s and 1980s, when the West started looking towards the East for spiritual guidance. Since yoga is a blend of physical, mental, and spiritual practices, more and more people started learning and practicing yoga regularly. Besides, immensely influential yoga teachers like B.K.S. Iyengar and Pattabhi Jois, among others, opened yoga schools, trained yoga teachers, taught millions of students and made yoga accessible to anybody wanting to learn it.

In the 21st century, yoga is more popular than it ever was. It is being promoted enthusiastically in India. And in the West, a lot of people swear by the benefits of yoga. In some circles, though, yoga has become fashionable—something that needs to be done to be 'in' with the crowd!

Acknowledgements

Writing this book was one of the most difficult things I've done, but it made me grow, both personally and as a writer. I'm grateful to Sudeshna Shome Ghosh, for believing that I'd be able to do this, and Radhika Shenoy, for steering the book gently to its completed state.

I imbibed the zeal for learning from my parents Brinda Rao and Nagraj Rao. This trait proved invaluable during research for this book. I don't know what I would've done without their unwavering support. My aunt Anu Jagalur always knows just what to say, and her keen eye makes my writing so much better. Thanks also to my extended family, for going over some parts of the book, for their suggestions, company, love and laughter.

Avani read the entire manuscript in its raw form

and offered pertinent and incisive suggestions—I'm both proud and awestruck. Grateful for her never-ending hugs that keep me going.

Finally, Sandesh, without whom this book wouldn't have been possible—thanks for adulting on my behalf.